THE OWL HOUSE

THE OWL HOUSE

DANIEL BUTLER

SEREN

Seren is the book imprint of
Poetry Wales Press Ltd,
Suite 6, 4 Derwen Road, Bridgend, Wales, CF31 1LH

www.serenbooks.com
facebook.com/SerenBooks
Twitter: @SerenBooks

ISBN: 9781781725061
Ebook: 9781781725047

A CIP record for this title is available from the British Library.

The publisher acknowledges the financial assistance
of the Welsh Books Council.

Cover photography by Geraint Evans.

Printed by Clays.

CONTENTS

Tan y Cefn	7
The House Owl	18
Birding Experiences	31
Welsh Weasels	42
Hawks	54
Spring Skies	65
Weather	81
Domestic Wildlife	105
Wildlife on the Move	116
History and Nature	123
Water	133
Farming Landscape	143
Welsh Raptors	149
Back from the Dead	159
Nature Does It Better	168
Autumn Bounty	175
The Hunting Drive	181
Cynefin	199
Acknowledgements	208

TAN Y CEFN

It was the views which sold the house: they were stunning. I'd always loved Wales, but I had no idea its heart was so spectacularly beautiful, so neglected and so wild. My pregnant partner, Bel, and I had been searching for a smallholding for three months, spending long weekends criss-crossing the Principality looking for the perfect place to raise a family and attempt the self-sufficient lifestyle which had been a dream since childhood.

The search for a Welsh smallholding was far more complex than a mere view. It also tied into my sense of ancestry, the urge to live in proximity to nature and, above all, it was driven by my passion for birds of prey. Anything with a hooked bill and talons triggered something deep inside – I yearned to be closer to nature.

Bel, might not have been as obsessive about hawks, falcons and owls, but she definitely shared my nesting urge and was fuelled by an increasing sense of urgency. Because I was a freelance journalist whose clients were London-based and she had spent almost all her life in West London, it seemed sensible to start our property search in the comparatively lush countryside of Monmouthshire and Herefordshire's Golden Valley. Nestling in the lee of the Black Mountains, this was beautifully rural, yet gave comparatively easy access to the motorway, family and work three hours to the east. The land here was rich and green, with flower-strewn meadows with cud-chewing cattle and meandering brooks. Overgrown hedges and neglected coppices framed each field and the banks of the watercourses were lined with the grey-green foliage of sallow and alder. This was wilder country than the rolling north Oxford-shire where I had spent my childhood – and nothing like Bel's Notting Hill.

The Golden Valley and the English end of the Brecon Beacons was an easy way to slip into a Welsh mind set – or rather that of the southern Marches. Unlike the Northern end of the Border, where accents and even language can transform suddenly in matter of miles, Herefordshire and Gloucestershire seem to blend seamlessly into Powys and Monmouthshire. Down here one side of the Severn or Wye seems much the same as the one opposite.

As we surveyed smallholdings around Abergavenny, I could easily imagine an idyllic existence here ... and yet as I glanced west, something tugged at me. This countryside was undoubtedly beautiful, but it seemed a little tame. I could certainly envisage my own version of *The Good Life*, raising a few animals here and tending a vegetable patch there, but my imagination was turbo-charged by the Romantics, thanks in large part to these being my academic mother's subject area. So when I mentally pictured my ideal home, I had visions of paintings by Martin and the poems of Wordsworth – the craggy vistas and open moors which would really set one's soul soaring. And there it seemed to be, just a few miles to the west, in the form of the Black Mountains and Brecon Beacons massif.

There was also the question of budget. We were trading in two very small mortgaged London flats for our rural idyll. Our city homes would buy a three-bedroom Monmouthshire home with three acres, but as we sifted through the estate agents' lists, it was clear we could get much more for our money by ranging deeper into Wales.

It was the early 1990s and deep housing recession was even deeper and darker in Wales. Its mountains and valleys seemed flooded with smallholdings for sale, most vacated by death and in probate. We looked at hundreds of properties: the bulk on paper only for generally it took only a moment's glance at the photocopied sheet or a minute or two to deem each unsuitable, but we also visited at least a couple of dozen.

The results were not encouraging. Many were totally impossible from the outset: in very poor condition or lacking the mains electricity and phone line necessary for a freelance journalist and a heavily pregnant first-time mother. Many were too close to a busy road and many were impossibly ugly or modern (UPVC windows were an automatic cause for rejection).

Our fastidiousness meant that the search started to go first further and further west and then to venture tentatively north. This was more like it! Or at least that was my reaction, but the hopelessly romantic homesteads high in the hills that caught my eye were either too pricey or too remote for Bel. She was more taken by Carmarthenshire and Pembrokeshire, drawn in large part by the proximity of comfortingly modern hospitals. On the other hand, I found the rolling countryside of the lush river plains with their dairy cows and arable fields too tame.

So we ranged out. As we went deeper into Wales the scenery and habitats became more spectacular and the wildlife possibilities more thrilling. The inclines were steeper, the skyline higher, and the woods bigger and older. Everything felt more deeply soaked in history. We looked at farms near first Brecon, then Llandovery. The landscape was scarred by a network of drovers' roads, largely lost and forgotten tracks that threaded across the hills from the pastures of Ceredigion to the prosperity of the Midlands with the almost limitless wealth of London beyond.

This was relatively unimportant as we searched for a home, but on a subconscious level the sense of history and tradition weighed heavily on my sense of ancestry. Both my parents were Oxford dons, but my mother's father came from humble, but very vague, Welsh roots. He was born out of wedlock at the turn of the twentieth century, his parentage as misty as an autumnal dawn in the Valleys.

Always the lover of a good story, he was reluctant to let reality get in the way of a funny tale, so every version of his upbringing was different from the last. He was certainly reared near Pontypridd and Caerphilly, but according to one of his versions of his upbringing, he was the result of an illicit liaison between a Tregaron milkmaid and her farmer boss. When the pregnancy became obvious, the farmer's wife was understandably furious and so, to hush things up, his mother moved to the coalfields of South Wales. There she met and married a policeman who became his official father. Subsequently it seemed more likely the policeman genuinely was his father, but whatever the truth, he certainly had many relatives near Newquay on the Ceredigion coast.

The picture starts to become clearer as he grew older. He definitely left school at fourteen, but was bright and rather than becoming a miner like his cousins, he briefly became a pit electrician. But working underground was not for him and he switched to work as an unqualified teacher. This was badly paid, so he supplemented his income by writing reports on births and deaths for the local paper. He was paid by the column inch, so wrote increasingly ornate descriptions of the latest funeral service. Eventually the sub-editors cut his flowery prose even more brutally than usual and he went to Cardiff to protest at his treatment, only to impress the editor with his gumption. This led to a full-time job as a reporter and he slowly worked his way up the ladder, via *The Manchester Guardian*, to end up as an industrial journalist in Fleet Street.

This ancestral tale cut little ice with Bel, but I definitely felt a sense of heritage as we drove through the hills. It was always at the back of my mind as we searched for a farmhouse where I could attempt my long-held dream of a self-sufficient lifestyle. I told myself that were I any sort of sportsman, I could use these roots to claim Welsh nationality and play in a red jersey.

I have to admit I took advantage of Bel's increasing morning sickness and apprehension about the approaching birth. She didn't seem to care too much about where we lived as long as we found somewhere. As a result our reconnaissance trips had a tendency to drift further north into the heart of Wales. Ostensibly I explained this was due to our limited budget: one could get so much more in this unfamiliar part of the world. In Monmouthshire we could afford a small detached house and a couple of acres. By the time we got to Builth that became four bedrooms, outhouses and five or six acres. Despite this, there always seemed to be something wrong when we arrived to view the latest property, until, that is, we spotted the details of a farm just outside a Radnorshire hamlet which neither of us had ever heard of.

We turned into the yard to find a south facing farm that sat bang on the 1100 foot contour. It was stone-built with thick walls and rough-hewn beams. Adjoining the house there was a semi-derelict long milking parlour while a couple of nineteenth century traditional barns stood across the lane. It came with about eleven acres of rough grazing, a small conifer plantation and duck pond.

The house had been on the market for two years and the vendors were clearly desperate to sell, not least because the wife was crippled by arthritic hips. As a result she wasn't able to join us outside, so Bel stayed indoors with her to drink tea and have a further poke around the dusty rooms. Meanwhile I walked around the land with her husband as he energetically emphasised its assets.

We walked into the field furthest from the house – five acres of steeply-sloping tussocky pasture. As I strode across the hillside, I couldn't help feeling that my host was oddly reluctant to carry on. Sensing a possible drawback I carried on for a few more yards to see huge mounds of fresh earth at the top of the bank just below the boundary fence.

'Badgers?' I asked.

'Yes, but they don't cause any problems,' he said hastily. 'Don't worry, there's no TB in the area.' This was clearly the cause of his reluctance to show me that corner of the property – he was terrified I might be planning on mixed livestock farming and badgers pose major headaches for cattle owners. That totally allayed my concerns – indeed it only boosted my enthusiasm for I had no intention of keeping cows. I have always loved 'Brock', although I had only seen a live Oxfordshire badger on two or three occasions. I was totally captivated by the property and was already starting to sketch out mental plans for improvements. Our host asked me what I did and what drew me to Radnorshire as we walked slowly back towards the plantation behind the house. I explained about the journalism and my obsessive interest in birds of prey. Now it was his turn to look excited. He sensed a valuable selling point.

'We've got owls here,' he said excitedly, pointing to a large box fastened to the huge oak growing on the edge of the plantation. 'There are tawnies hooting all the time and I've even seen barn owls down the lane in the headlights.'

'Do the barn owls breed here?' I asked.

For a moment he hesitated, clearly itching to say they did, but then he shook his head, perhaps suspecting that in my enthusiasm I might clamber around the barns looking for evidence of pellets or droppings. In fact it didn't matter too much to me: the mere hint it might be possible just poured more fuel on my already wildly enflamed imagination. By the time I got back to the house I was determined to put in an offer.

And as we stood talking to the owners before leaving, I could sense Bel had also fallen for the place. It was a gorgeous day and the views were at their best. The farm looks south down the Wye Valley. In the distance, beyond the ridge of the Mynydd Eppynt, the hilly wilderness between Builth Wells and Brecon, the twin peaks of Pen y Fan were visible and to the east I could make out the distinctive almost geometric escarpment of Hay Bluff. To the west was a spectacular glacial bowl behind the village of Llanwrthwl which promised fantastic walking.

The house was called Tan y Cefn. This sounded wildly romantic, but when I asked my mother she pointed out that like most Welsh place names, it has a remarkably prosaic translation simply meaning 'back of the hill'. This made perfect sense because it nestles in a sheltered nook (originally a Welsh word 'cnwch') on the south side of the protective mass of Gwasteddyn. This is the mountain that looms over the market town of Rhayader on its northern flank. A 1650 foot peak marks its western end, while a two-mile long 1500 foot high plateau stretches eastwards. Tan y Cefn is about halfway along the southern side of the mountain, sheltered from the worst of the wind and rain by being some 400 foot below the pastures above.

After finishing our inspection it took just one glance between us to realise we had found the house of our dreams. All the same we said little to each other, but agreed it would be sensible to see what the local town was like. We took the back road into Rhayader, driving along a narrow lane that curves along the hillside some 200 feet above the main road below. As we rounded the corner to look west and north found stunning views towards the Elan Valley and north towards Pumlumon. The latter is both the highest point in

Mid-Wales and also its largest catchment and the source of not only the Wye, but the Severn and Rheidol. A moment later I spotted a buzzard floating above the wood below.

I stopped the car to stare at the sight and was mesmerised by the beauty of the near stationary bird which hung in the air just a few yards to my right. I was utterly fascinated by the sight of the feathers on its back ruffling in the headwind. Buzzards are often largely ignored by bird lovers as relatively drab brown hawks. They are often anthropomorphically dismissed as 'lazy' because although they certainly can hunt actively, generally they prefer carrion or small fare – voles, beetles and even worms and larvae, plucked from upturned cowpats. This does little justice to what is actually a master of the skies, a hawk capable of soaring effortlessly for hours on end. In theory this is hunting, scouring the fields hundreds, sometimes thousands, of feet below for rodents or fallen stock, but if one watches the birds circling way overhead on a breezy cloudless day one can't help feeling they also fly purely for enjoyment – entering a reverie as they surf the invisible thermals and air currents on motionless unfurled wings. That morning we both sat entranced for at least two or three minutes before it wheeled away and shot off downwind. I couldn't help thinking there might be better places in the United Kingdom to find birds of prey – but there aren't many and certainly none closer to London.

Rhayader is situated in what is very definitely at the heart of Wales: a place near the point where the Welsh-speaking west and north meet the anglophone South and East. This is the tipping point between the Brecon Beacons and Snowdonia, halfway between England and Cardigan Bay at Wales's narrowest point. Yet in many ways this seems to exist in a vacuum in the popular imagination. This is the forgotten Wales, the 'hole in the doughnut' as some have put it.

Few people outside the Principality have heard of Rhayader – certainly neither Bel nor I had until we found Tan y Cefn – thus for a quarter of a century I have had to describe the location to others as the transaction point of a giant imaginary cross drawn from Chester to St David's and from Chepstow to Anglesey: either that or as being the halfway point between Hereford and Aberystwyth.

Rhayader's anglicised name is derived from Rhaeadr Gwy – 'Waterfall on the Wye'. Until the end of the eighteenth century there were impressive falls on the river which hems it in to the west. These were blown up to allow the construction of a bridge, linking the town with the tiny village of Cwmdauddwr ('Valley of the Two Waters') which lies on the other side of the river. Otherwise it is at the least populated end of Radnorshire, which is in turn the least populated county in England and Wales. Its name derives from a thuggish follower of William the Conqueror a thuggish monarch who controlled his equally violent and greedy followers by granting them large sections of rebellious territory along the Marches. They were given carte blanche to whip the troublesome Celts into submission.

In theory Radnorshire no longer exists for it was swallowed up in the 1970s administrative reorganisations to become the middle section of Powys, sandwiched between Montgomery to the north and Brecknock to the south. It may have been abolished as a county in the 1970s, but it still very definitely exists as far as locals are concerned. To the east it touches Shropshire and Hereford, while to the west it rises to form the Cambrian Mountains, with the coastal strip of Ceredigion beyond.

But to return to the practicalities of the area: both the main north to south roads of Wales, those from Swansea to Chester and Cardiff to Caernarfon run through this tiny county Another historic highway, the old coach road from London and the South Midlands to Aberystwyth, slashes right to left across Wales at this point, although today this is little used except by touring bikers and tourists. It is not a Welsh-speaking area, although this changes only a few miles to the rural north and west. This was a mild disappointment, for it is a beautiful and ancient language, although it is still very much alive across the whole Principality in the form of place names. For example my neighbours are at Esgair Rhiw ('long ridge'), Pen Ffynon ('top spring') and Nantglas ('blue stream').

As I looked at the views and listened to the sounds of high summer, I was sure I could be happy here, that we could settle in and make ourselves truly at home. Cynefin is the Welsh word for 'hefted': the ancient form of upland farming. Its roots are in a Neolithic age when flocks of sheep, goats and cattle roamed the open hills, unfettered by boundary hedges or walls. The animals were left largely to their own devices from spring to autumn because although there was nothing to stop them wandering for many miles, they felt secure in familiar surroundings. They knew every fold of the land: where best to take shelter from a biting north wind, the choicest grazing and the most reliable springs in the driest of summers. This was something they had learnt from their parents: knowledge passed down the generations.

The same sense of rootedness pervades Wales's human inhabitants. There is a strong sense of belonging to the locality which over-rides loyalties to a county, the Principality, let alone the United Kingdom. It was ever thus. Wales was never a kingdom, but at best a group of fiefdoms ruled by warrior princes. Ask a Welshman where they're from and the answer will almost always be the local town or even village. From the moment I had seen the house, its fields and its views, I felt I could establish my own cynefin here – that I could put down roots and become as locked into the area as firmly as mountain ewes grazing on the moors of the Elan Valley.

This urge to bind myself to the surrounding landscape, to its fields, woods and rocks was only strengthened by the tiny life growing inside Bel. The baby's arrival was, appropriately enough, at Easter just as local ewes would be lambing in the fields behind the house while the hedges would begin to ring with the calls of thousands of songbirds that would flood in from Africa.

HOUSE OWL

It was in late spring that first year that I caught my first really good view of a barn owl. Although I knew they were present from the occasional glimpse in the car headlights down on the main roads, it was several months before I saw one actually hunting around the farm.

I had gone out hoping to see badger cubs on a glorious May evening, so even though the sun was about to set and it was comparatively late; there was still almost an hour of light left. It was warm and the light was soft and had that wonderful golden glow of a low sun casting long shadows across the land. I toiled up the steep slope towards the sett, skirting up the side of the conifer plantation before walking west along the contour, trying to make as little noise as possible. I kept the prevailing breeze in my face and my camera, complete with telephoto lens, was set for the light and with a quick shutter speed.

The long grass was warm as I sank down on the hillside, revelling in the spectacular views down the Wye Valley, over the Eppynt ranges between Builth and Brecon, towards the distant Pen y Fan. The air was full of the thick, slightly musty scent of pollen. To start with there was nothing but bird song. This was already starting to calm down from the frenzy of a month earlier, but a few males were still bothering to proclaim their territories. I sank into the grass, lapping up the smells, sounds and sights of a heavenly evening. After twenty minutes or so, I was rewarded by movement some thirty yards away. It came from a hillside hole but it was not badgers, instead a cascade of four fox cubs. They were playing at the entrance of an earth that had once been a rabbit burrow. I raised my camera ever so slowly and clicked away. For ten minutes I was entranced as they rolled and tumbled around the dusty earth their mother had presumably scratched out in spring as she enlarged the burrow.

Eventually the cubs noticed my presence and scrambled back underground. I turned to look down the hill, the sunset to my right and the Brecon Beacons in front. The hill was bathed in the warm orange light of the now-vanished sun reflected off the handful of clouds overhead. I felt an inner glow – this was my hillside and these were my views. I lay down, sinking beneath the grass seed heads to bask in the scenery and the calls of songbirds settling down for the night. My nostrils were filled too with delicate scents of pollen, and bumble bees buzzed over the grass around me. Two large black beetles struggled across the tussocks, making heavy weather of the long blades, but obviously intent on some destination – maybe a hole or dung pile. A few gatekeeper butterflies flittered over the grass and in the distance a tractor was chugging. I lay back on the grass and stared at the heavens. It was one of those days where the sky – while still bright – contained the moon and Venus was starting to be visible as a faint pin-prick just above the western horizon.

And then the owl appeared – a large white form floating silently across the hillside on steady wing beats. Well, I say 'white', which is how a barn owl normally appears when glimpsed at night and particularly so when this is in the beam of a torch, for it is the pure white of the underside and face which catch the light best. But in the dwindling daylight this evening, I was much more struck by quite how golden its upper feathers appeared. Anyone who has seen a barn owl close up will know its 'mantle' is a glorious soft yellow, interspersed with greys and light browns and dotted with tiny black spots. It was the golden upper parts that caught the dying light best and it positively seemed to glow, particularly each time she wheeled around to make another pass above the silvery seed heads which rippled in the lightest of breezes.

I sat absolutely motionless as the owl quartered back and forth across the slope. It flew steadily and with buoyant wing beats, her head directed towards the ground, clearly totally absorbed by the search for field voles. I was hypnotised as it flew methodically back and forth, floating over the sward in search of prey. Barely daring to breathe I raised the camera and pressed the shutter button. Nothing happened – I had fired off my entire roll of film taking pictures of the fox cubs. So instead I had to sit motionless as the owl flew with bouncing silent wing beats above the grass.

Barn and short-eared owls are much more active hunters than our other three mainland species. Tawny, long-eared and little owls generally still-hunt: that is to say they perch on a suitable vantage point such as a branch or post and wait for prey to venture into range. In contrast short-eared owls and barn owls hunt by patrolling back and forth across open ground. The first generally prefer moors, heaths and coastal marshes, although they will also hunt in farmland, while barn owls are most likely to be found hunting on rough pasture. Both certainly have wonderful sight, but they are actually hunting predominantly by sound – detecting scurrying quarry by the rustling of grass, heather or fern.

As I watched this quartering barn owl, I decided this was better than any Attenborough documentary because this was reality and I was watching it in my field. The colours of late spring were superb too – if only I hadn't used my film! The golden wings, white undersides and silvery grass heads were almost ethereal, supernatural, against the contrasting worldly background of the vibrant greens of an early Welsh summer. It was magical: a scene which will live with me forever.

And then it swooped, diving into the ankle-high grass. It stayed there, frozen, for what seemed like minutes, but was probably no more than ten seconds. Half its body was hidden from view, so I couldn't tell if it had been successful. I waited: if it had caught it would do one of two things – wolf down its prize or take it back to a brood. After what felt like an age, it bent down and then a moment later lifted into the air. As it flew off, I thought I glimpsed something small and dark in its feet, but couldn't be sure. Nevertheless, it was heading back towards the house. I leaped to my feet and ran after it – obviously fruitlessly – because I lost sight within seconds, but the idea that it might have a nest nearby was thrilling.

These days almost everyone loves these nocturnal hunters, but this benign attitude is rather different from our superstitious forebears. They viewed these creatures with a mixture of fear and suspicion.

Os y ddylluan ddaw i're fro
Lle byddo rhywun afiach
Dod yno i ddweyd y mae' ddinad
Na chaiff adferiad mwyach

If an owl visits
Where someone sick is lying
It is to say without a doubt
The invalid is dying

It is perhaps not too difficult to see why owls might sometimes be viewed with unease: these ghostly white birds usually appear without warning, floating silently into view. Also, often the first indications of their presence are sinister hisses from the depths of an outbuilding – sounds far more suited to a cursing witch than a beautiful hunter. And yet at the same time our ancestors could value them too. Barns were built with apertures near the eaves to encourage owls to take up residence to control rodents in the grain stores and they were welcomed in church steeples too.

The sight of the owl and the knowledge that the owls appreciated nesting in buildings inspired me to do some DIY. I looked up designs for owl boxes in one of the myriad of bird-related books I'd bought in Hay-on-Wye soon after our arrival. The designs were simple enough – basically a homemade wooden tea chest with a six-inch entrance hole. I then made a trip to the local building supplies to buy wood, only to spot a pile of pallets by the gate. These were free to any customer prepared to take them away, so I manhandled three into the back of our canvass-topped long wheel-based Land Rover and bought a pound of nails. Returning home, I dismantled the pallets to produce a pile of planks and then spent a happy morning measuring, sawing and hammering to create a big box. This was not a thing of beauty (I am not a natural joiner), but I figured the owls wouldn't care: they normally nest in cavities in old trees or dusty wall tops in barns and outbuildings.

When I had finished, I picked a spot to mount it in the barn opposite the study window. I chose one of the A frames supporting the roof and with the aid of a rope and a crude pulley, managed to haul it into position. After a lot of swearing, several near-accidents and bruised fingers, I secured it just below the slates with half a dozen six inch nails. It remained there, unused, for several years. Each autumn I would clamber up to check on occupancy, but there were no signs of nesting – or even that it had been visited. After five years or so I largely forgot about it, not least because further owl sightings were confined to those momentary glimpses of a white form in the car headlights.

The owls stubbornly ignored the box for year upon year and the real breakthrough came five or six years later. I had heard of a wildlife photographer and bird ringer operating locally and wondered whether I might profile him for an article. This was of course really just an excuse to pick his brains on local wildlife highlights. I phoned for a chat and we arranged to meet at the kite feeding station on the other side of our hill that evening. I drove over and was chatting away cheerfully when a tearful delivery driver screeched into the yard. He had just clipped an owl with his van on a local lane. He was distraught and described the accident as if it had been a child running out into the road from between parked cars.

'It just appeared from nowhere, flew across the lane in front of me,' he gasped. 'I couldn't brake – didn't have a chance. I hit it with the corner of my windscreen.'

It doesn't take much to damage the delicate bones of a bird. These are built to be as light as possible and although strengthened by an internal honeycomb structure, even a light blow will cause a break. The photographer and I gave each other knowing looks. Anyone who's had any experience of rehabilitation knows a broken wing effectively rules out a return to the wild for it will never be as good as before. Barn owls live on the edge at the best of times. They need to be perpetually at the peak of fitness to survive because their style of hunting is very active, quartering slowly and silently above pastures which requires the absolute peak of fitness and condition. Every muscle and bone must be perfect – anything less and the survival seesaw tips in favour of the prey. Yet we could not voice this in front of the driver who desperately needed reassurance. And while I was sure it would be a death sentence to release the bird, even if it were to apparently be capable of flight, it would quickly starve to death in the wild. Yet euthanizing such a beautiful bird seemed a crime, so it was destined to spend its life in an aviary. Or in this case it took the form of the end of my barn, hastily adapted by fitting mesh and bars over the windows.

By pure chance I was given another owl a month later. This was captive-bred and was owned by a falconer in very poor health. I was short of space, so I put them in the same pen, for barn owls are not nearly so aggressive towards each other as tawnies. Also, although it is difficult to sex barn owls, males tend to be paler and spots on the flanks usually denote a female. I thought I detected a difference in colour between this pair and one seemed to have flecks on her sides, so I reckoned there was at least a fifty-fifty chance they were a pair. Sure enough, they were soon sitting on eggs and that summer produced three clutches and fledging seven owlets in all.

I could have slipped on numbered closed rings when they were a week old and applied for paperwork to prove they were captive bred. I could then have sold them, but owls don't make good pets as I was discovering. I wasn't getting any pleasure simply looking at the pair hunched on a beam. Owls and hawks are made to fly and to hunt and these did little apart from eat and breed. So in the end I gave the adult pair to a friend, but this left me with the problem of what to do with the young. The deliberate release of captive-bred owls is prohibited, but I figured that as these were the offspring of a local bird, it was within the spirit of rehabilitation ethics to treat them as wild so I cut a hole in the wire and after a day or two the residents left. I continued to put food in the aviary and this regularly disappeared although I had no idea whether this was down to the owls or a rat.

A couple of months later my son reported an owl had attacked his tennis ball as he was playing on the lawn. I went out to check and sure enough there was a barn owl perched on one of the posts that made up our fruit cage, apparently unconcerned by our proximity, but staring intently at the fluffy yellow ball on the grass beneath. I had been defrosting chicks for my hawks, so I tossed one out and the owl swooped down. Over the following months it got progressively tamer, eventually coming to the front door when called.

That winter it paired with a truly wild native and next summer they produced one clutch of three (young birds are much less likely to produce multiple clutches than older birds). The next year the female laid eight eggs in one batch (I had cautiously climbed up for a very brief inspection during the incubation). This meant the last chick would be a fortnight younger than its oldest sibling, so in an effort to protect it from cannibalism, I put out up to twenty chicks each evening

It paid off. All eight chicks fledged and for a brief period at dusk the farmyard resembled a scene from Harry Potter with white forms dotted around roofs or perched on the children's climbing frame. Unfortunately something must have happened to the tame owl that winter, because for the next ten years the farm was apparently owl-less. No doubt there were others – they might even have bred here – but I saw very few owls over the next decade, although droppings and pellets showed that we had at least the occasional visitor. The lack of sightings was not that surprising, for despite being large, pale and active at dawn and dusk, barn owls are remarkably elusive: they are very good at tucking themselves away in dark corners by day and flying off quickly and silently to their hunting grounds.

One chilly evening in late spring I went out to try to photograph a particularly stunning night sky. This can be truly amazing and on a clear night often leaves visitors gaping open mouthed in wonder. The lack of people means there is very little light pollution, indeed the Elan Valley has been designated an International Dark Skies Park. Even at first glance the heavens were awash with tiny pricks of light. As I stared slowly more and more dots appeared until my mind began to swim with the enormity of it all.

There is a line in one of my favourite children's books, *Brendon Chase* by B.B., where one of the protagonists, a fourteen-year-old boy, is lying on his back next to a campfire staring up at the stars, imagining that each one is a distant person. Then the enormity of it all dawns on him and the smallness of his own being seems terrifying and he has to roll back to focus on the comforting burning embers instead. As I looked up, I suddenly had the same sense of the infinite insignificance of my own existence, but I carried on staring up, trying to identify the handful of constellations that I can recognise without a book.

I stood in silence for what felt like an age, but was returned to reality when I heard a strange sound from the barn opposite: the hissing, snoring call that I'd last heard several years before. I went back out with a torch and tip-toed to the barn. It now seems ridiculous that I might imagine I could creep in undetected by a bird with one of the most acute senses of hearing in the natural world, one able to detect a vole scurrying beneath dense grass. Nevertheless I tried. Sure enough there was silence as I crept across the lane, but when I shone the torch up into the eaves, I was rewarded with a brief flash of white as the owl fled the building.

I hastily put up another feeding platform outside the living room window and every evening put out a couple of the defrosted day-old chicks that I buy by the thousand for the hawks. I didn't see or hear the owl again for a month, although sometimes the chicks disappeared. More often than not, they didn't and even when they were gone the next morning, there was no way to tell what had taken them – it could have been one of the tawny owls that were calling every evening or, for that matter, an early morning magpie.

Then one evening I saw her sitting on the table waiting for me to come out with the evening feed. Naturally she flew off as soon as I opened the door, so I put out the food, went back inside and waited and a few minutes later she was there. It was a fleeting visit, pausing on the table for only a second – just long enough to grab a chick in her beak and fly off. Within an hour the other two chicks had gone too.

The pattern was repeated the next evening – the owl was there waiting as I opened the door and this time she paused momentarily before fleeing. This happened again and again over the next week, each time she seemed to linger longer on the table. After a few days I stopped when I opened the door and as the owl remained on the table, instead of advancing towards her, I held out my hand, a chick on my palm.

The owl refused to come, but there was a distinct hesitation. On a whim I held back the rations that night. The following evening it was there again. I held out my hand and the owl sat there, some three metres away, bobbing its head up and down repeatedly. This is just how a hawk in the early stages of training behaves. It indicates it wants the food, but is struggling to overcome its instinctive suspicion of a human. Eventually the owl opened its wings and fell off the table towards me, pausing for only a split second on my hand before flying off with the chick in its mouth.

It was a critical breakthrough and one I was not going to let slip. The next evening I was at the door with another chick in my outstretched palm. After a while there was a slight thump from the other side of the yard as the owl landed on the sill of the barn's unglazed window. It stared at me for what seemed and age, but didn't approach and then retreated into the darkness of the building. The next day, however, it was emboldened by hunger and floated across the lane to land on the rail in front of the house. It sat there, bobbing its head, close enough for me to admire the golden plumage spotted with tiny black flecks and hints of grey. And then it launched itself towards me, once more landing lightly on my hand, the talons pricking my palm. They felt like needles pressed lightly into the skin: mildly uncomfortable, but leaving no mark. This was only for the briefest of moments, however, and then it was off before flying off across the lane to the reassuring shelter of the barn.

This became a routine and I found it surprisingly easy to get it coming in steadily. Within a week it was a predictable occurrence within a few minutes of sunset. This certainly felt marvellous, but in a way it was less surprising than one might think. After all, the principles are those used by falconers for several millennia. In fact this was easier than the falconry I'd been practicing for several years. I didn't need to bother weighing the bird, let alone fumble with jesses and radio tracking devices. The owl rapidly became increasingly reliable. It would now pause on my outstretched palm for long enough for me to examine it in greater detail. Although there is no discernible size difference between the sexes and ostensibly very little when it comes to barn owl plumage, there was just enough mottling on the flanks to persuade me 'it' was probably 'she'.

Soon after I heard distinctive hissing sounds from the barn as she landed on my palm. Clearly she had a mate and the pair were building up to copulation and laying! Her growing tameness was probably down to her increasing nutritional requirements required by a laying female which would partially explain her willingness to overcome her natural fear to come to first the table and then my hand. I waited for a fortnight and then cautiously clambered up to inspect the tea chest of a nest box that I had manhandled into the eaves of the barn several years before. As I reached the entrance I was almost knocked off the ladder in surprise by a burst of soft white feathers exploding past my face as the incubating mother left the nest. I peered in, anxious not to spend a moment longer than necessary, and was rewarded by the sight of six white eggs.

The first of these hatched in early May and over the course of the next week it was joined by three more chicks. This in itself is one of those small details which reveals just another wonderful solution to the infinitely complex and perilous survival strategies that birds have evolved over countless millennia. Most species only begin to incubate their eggs when they have completed laying the entire clutch. They want their young to hatch at the same time to minimise squabbles within the nest. Indeed in many cases the chicks co-operate with this strategy, cheeping to each other from within the egg to let their siblings know they are about to hatch and this can actually spur on the latecomers.

Barn owls adopt a very different approach. The female starts to incubate as soon as the first egg is laid and the youngsters grow very fast, so the smallest chick might fit into a teaspoon while its oldest sibling could be almost as big as its parents. This staggered hatching is fine in a good year for voles, but can be grim news for the youngest in times of dearth when its older siblings will readily recycle the available protein: cannibalism is common.

I kept close tabs on our clutch, although I strictly rationed my visits to the nest, climbing up only once a week. Four of the six eggs hatched and once again I made sure to put out double or even treble rations of food every evening in an attempt to insulate the smallest from any urge for a canapé on the part of their larger siblings. Whenever I checked the nest, the young birds would hiss and clatter their beaks in outraged protest as I peered in. As time went on I would be almost knocked off the ladder by the stench which was a powerful mix of rotting meat and ammonia from the nitrogen-rich droppings. I was providing up to a dozen chicks a day and the mother would take them all. No doubt much of the stench in the nest was due to stashed yellow corpses, but judging from the numerous grey-black pellets scattered around the garage and barn, the owls – both adult and young – were supplementing their chick diet with plenty of voles and mice.

Indeed, I dismantled several to see what they were eating by putting them in a bowl of water and after a few minutes and a quick stir, I poured the contents onto a sheet of kitchen paper and pulled out a magnifying glass to examine the loose grey brown paste. Scraping the mass of fur to one side, I was left with a mass of indeterminate small bones, supplemented with skulls and jaws. These were easier to identify. The broader skulls came from voles, the narrower ones came from mice and those with sharp teeth were from shrews. My owls were clearly dining better on the local wildlife than they were on my chicks, for there was almost no trace of yellow fluff in the pellets.

BIRDING EXPERIENCES

One early formative interest had come soon after our arrival. My obsessive interest in birds of prey led me to go to an evening talk on red kites by Iolo Williams. He is now a nationally known broadcaster, but was then working for the RSPB and effectively responsible for rare birds across Wales. A quarter of a century later kites are ubiquitous across most of Wales and much of lowland England, but at this point they were definitely near the top of his list of priorities. I tentatively asked if I might write something about him for one of the nationals and – with an eye to the favourable publicity for the charity – he readily agreed.

With the benefit of hindsight, my house's location probably helped because at the time it stood at the top edge of the kite's last British stronghold. Also during the early 1990s the RSPB and army were co-operating to protect the Elan Valley's two nests and Iolo could see the opportunity for highlighting what was really a mutual PR exercise for both charity and military.

With the benefit of hindsight, I doubt there was any real point in giving a remote nest a 24-hour guard. Although the Victorians were passionate about egg collecting and it was still rife during the first half of the twentieth century, the number of egg collectors went into sharp decline after the Second World War. By the 1990s numbers had dwindled to a handful, so the chances of a thief picking the only guarded nest out of Wales's eighty-odd was extremely remote. The chances were even further reduced by the nest being sited at the end of a long valley with only one access road. Any potential thief could be easily trapped with a car parked across the road. But these days conservation is so much about appearances. This exercise showed the world that the RSPB was fighting for Wales's threatened raptors and that the army cared about conservation and the environment.

Iolo and I met in Rhayader car park and drove up the valley in my ancient Land Rover, chatting as we went. I noticed at three or four points he broke off our chat to stare intently upwards. The reason became clear at the last when he barked out a command to stop. I did so and we got out to stare at a bird high above us. It was momentarily motionless, hanging in the air as it faced into the wind – and then it was off, wings beating fast as it powered towards the horizon.

'Was that?...' My voice trailed off.

'Yep: peregrine,' said Iolo.

I was thrilled to the core. I had never seen a peregrine before and had put them on a mental pedestal as one of Britain's rarest predators. In fact they are far from rare, although in common with all top predators, by definition they are in low numbers relative to their prey. Nevertheless, to any European falconer this is the absolute pinnacle of all raptors. In fact that probably goes for most bird-lovers. This is the fastest living creature and one of the largest falcons in the world, exceeded in size only by the Arctic hunting gyrfalcon and its close relative, the saker, which ranges the vast steppes of southern Russia and Kazakhstan.

Back at home the local tawny owls were still very vocal. From the sound of it we were on the border of two territories, for 'too whit, too woos' were coming from either side of the house every night. These seemingly gentle calls are actually at the extreme end of avian aggression. Tawny owls are incredibly belligerent for their relatively diminutive size. Weighing about the same as a pack of butter, they will tackle prey as large as a big rat or half-grown rabbit and are just as feisty with rivals or anything they think might be attacking their young. Indeed, their own offspring prefer to jump out of the nest as soon as they can rather than live with their siblings – which accounts for the large number of 'abandoned' owlets brought in to vets and rescue centres in early summer. In reality they are far from orphaned, for their parents know exactly where they are and quietly return to feed them throughout the night.

The tawny's aggression is not limited to its own kind. The great wildlife photographer Eric Hoskings lost his left eye to a tawny owl which attacked him at the nest. I knew this because as a child I had watched him regularly on *Animal Magic*. His conversations with Johnny Morris were memorable, not least because Hoskings looked positively piratical with his eye patch. He had been born in the North London suburbs just before the First World War, but grew up with a love of nature and is credited as the first professional bird photographer. He was handicapped by slow film speeds and equipment which was primitive in the extreme by today's standards, yet he his knowledge of wildlife and natural instinct for composition made his name.

It was he who took an early iconic photo of a barn owl which most people have probably seen, even if they don't give him the credit. The owl is photographed head on as it flies into the nest through an opened aperture; its wings outstretched back and up. It looks like an angel. I can't be alone in being totally entranced by that image – the perfect wildlife photo which blends great field craft with spot-on timing and yet also resonates with human culture. Hoskings told Morris it had taken him 365 shots before everything came together with this snap. In those days flash guns were powered by magnesium bulbs which went off with a loud 'pop' whenever the shutter was fired and needed to be physically replaced between each photograph. How on earth he managed to persuade a pair of wild owls to put up with this is beyond me.

Thanks to the conversations on the *Animal Magic* sofa, I knew that Hoskings had lost the eye to an owl strike, but it wasn't until Iolo told me the story that I realised how close this was to home. In 1937 he had set up a hide at the end of my little valley – literally within sight of my smallholding – to photograph a pair of tawnies. These were nesting in a cavity at the top of a tall tree. Hoskins had laboriously constructed a scaffolding tower opposite the nest and would arrive with a friend. They would ascend the tower and then the friend would leave, the idea being that because owls can't count, they wouldn't realise the hide was still occupied.

This went on for a few days, but after one long fruitless session, Hoskins gave up for the night and descended to go home, leaving his equipment in the hide. As he reached his car he thought he heard voices. He was worried these might be poachers or ne'er-do-wells, so he decided to return to retrieve his cameras. As he reached the platform, one of the adult birds flew at him and skewered his retina. The wound went sceptic and the photographer was left him with the option of losing one eye or risking total blindness were the infection to reach the optic nerve (these were pre-penicillin days). He opted to have his damaged eye removed and for the rest of his life wore an eye-patch.

As spring progressed that first year, I embarked on a steep avian learning curve. The action began in February with the first really noisy daytime territorial songs. Well, sing might be a generous description of the honking rattle of the ravens. I was well-used to the sight of crows, rooks and jackdaws, but the display flights of the huge black birds were new to me. These birds of ill-omen, which followed marauding armies along the Marches to feast on battlefield corpses, are usually loners, but in spring they start to fly in tandem.

As they rowed on creaking wings through the air, they would suddenly fold their wings and flip around in the air in what looks like an air ace's victory roll, barrelling through the skies to impress their mates. And all the while the pair would give throaty croaks reminiscent of a Mexican drum rattle: beads battering against taut parchment.

At about the same point the kites start to display in earnest, circling lazily on stiff wings above promising trees and launching occasional mock stoops on potential rivals. Once the pair has decided on a site – usually in late March or early April, they can build a nests amazingly quickly, taking just two or three days to create the two-foot-wide platform in a fork towards the top of a tall tree. That said, in general they seem to prefer to refurbish an old crow's nest, adding a few new twigs certainly, but more significantly they always adorn their would-be nursery with wool. Sometimes they will even add scraps of plastic for extra decoration (the recent pink wrap to sponsor breast cancer research is particularly appreciated).

This is the failsafe way to work out a nest's occupant, because ravens and buzzards are not interested in such trinkets. Quite why kites need to accessorise is a mystery, but the urge is clearly deep-rooted. In Shakespeare's *A Winter's Tale*, Autolycus warns: "When the kite builds, look to lesser linen." This is presumably because urban kites, deprived of ready supplies of wool, would snatch smaller scraps of fabric such as underwear from washing lines.

The main influx of birds intent on reproduction comes a couple of months later as thousands of migrant songbirds touched down from Africa. The first are the chiffchaffs soon to be joined by a plethora of other species.

Much as I love the start of the dawn chorus season, the real high points of my spring birding come around the end of April. First to arrive is the redstart. Until I moved here I had never seen one of these colourful migrants with their flashing red tails and the males clown-like black and white head and orange chest. My first sighting was pure enchantment!

As I washed the dishes one morning I looked up to see a gaudy clown perched on the washing line outside and making darting dives into the newly-mown grass below. It was one of the most colourful native birds I'd seen. They were once found all over Britain, but are now confined to western Britain, with outposts in West Coast Scotland and Cumbria, but with their greatest stronghold in Mid-Wales.

Indeed Iolo once remarked quietly that while the red kite might be the county bird of Powys and it certainly represented a conservation triumph, the redstart would actually be a better icon: 'You can easily see kites anywhere these days,' he said. 'But the keen birders come here for the redstarts and pied flycatchers. This is the best place to see both.' I could see his point. Thanks to reintroductions and natural recovery I now see kites almost all the way along my regular drives from Mid-Wales to Oxford and even as far as London – or at least the M25.

I therefore look forward every spring to my first redstart. For some reason this usually occurs in the same place – at a bend halfway up our access road – and the first concrete proof is invariably the flash of a red tail bouncing along the lane in front. Oddly, the first birds are usually the rather drabber females, but soon the more gaudy males are present. These are the ones that definitely catch the eye.

The first swallow is another highlight. These arrive elsewhere in Britain – even Wales – before Easter, but generally the first sighting in the farmyard will be in early May when a solitary traveller starts to flit back and forth, feeding up as it waits for companions to arrive. These fast-flying aerial acrobats are as impressive as any falcon, cavorting through the air as they hunt insects. More heart-lifting is their sheer exuberance and joie de vivre, once the first is joined by others. Despite their 8,000 mile flight from South Africa, they celebrate the start of their breeding season with a gorgeous babble of excited song, a flowing torrent of notes that gushes out as they dart back and forth over the lawn. The outpourings grow ever more frenetic as they flick in and out of the barns to inspect possible nest sites as full of irresponsible joie de vivre as a gang of twenty year-olds on a hen night.

Not for nothing is their full common name the barn swallow for they are irresistibly drawn to buildings, pulled to open doors and windows as if dragged by a magnet. Unlike barn owls which are happy to rear their young in hollow trees, swallows have become totally dependent on man for nest sites and always choose the shelter of a man-made structure. They have been doing this for thousands of years for they are depicted in Egyptian tomb murals, so at about the same time that the first humans were probing their way into Wales, swallows were nesting in man's earliest brick structures.

The urge to explore buildings for suitable nest sites on ledges or beams, particularly early in the season, inevitably leads them to discover the perching owls, resulting in a torrent of chattering outrage. Then the swooping sickle-winged birds hurtle in and out of the barn, calling out to others to join them in mobbing this lurking white danger.

The guides generally don't classify swallows as songbirds, yet my heart always lifts at the sheer happiness of these dark blue-backed, red-throated, white-chested, swallow-tailed hunters – they seem to be a cross between an opera diva and a flying ace. Also, while they might not have hooked beak and talons, they are aerial hunters every bit as capable and agile as a merlin or peregrine. Their prey might be near-invisible tiny insects, but they swoop and dart back and forth with a total mastery of the skies. They prefer to hunt low, flicking over the lawn or hay fields to catch flies and insects just above the grass, hurtling at blistering speed only inches above certain destruction. One mistake, one wing clipping the turf, would probably spell a broken bone and death – but within days of leaving the nest they are all at it. They seem to thrive on the challenge of the risk and love to show off their skills, daring each other to fly faster and lower. Their distant cousins, the house martins, arrive two or three weeks later to build cupped nests of mud under the eaves. These are more substantial than the swallows' flimsy ledges inside the barn or garage, but they are every bit as sociable. They also hunt in a different manner, tending to hunt at a higher altitude, flying together in darting flocks two or three hundred feet above the farm.

One of my favourite local songsters is unfortunately generally only heard for two or three days in mid-May. This is the babbling cry of the curlew calling from the wetlands in the valley below. These are one of our largest waders: only a little smaller than an egret, but unlike these brilliant white new arrivals, curlews are a drab brown, although clearly identifiable in flight with their long curved bills and trailing legs. Every year on a late spring morning the bubbling cry floats up from the rushy ground a few hundred yards down the valley. It is both beautiful and yet mournful too and sadly, every year the calls last barely a week before they cease abruptly.

Curlews are yet another of those upland birds whose numbers now appear to be in freefall. Agricultural changes are often blamed, but this can't be the whole story. Most of the soggy sheep-grazed pastures have been farmed in the same manner for centuries. Certainly many have been drained and are over-grazed, making worms harder to find and reducing cover, thus exposing their nests and young to predators. Yet there is still plenty of unimproved land where conditions are largely unchanged.

An increase in predators, particularly the opportunists, is probably most to blame locally. I rose early one May morning to revel in the dawn chorus. The sky was blue and the air was crisp, but even though it was still cold, the light breeze felt warmer because it was filled with the promise of a glorious day to come. It was also rich with the scents of late spring – the cut grass from the previous evening's mowing and nectar from the first flowers of the year. The worker bees from the hives behind the house were humming gently in the sycamores next to the garage, gathering pollen from the dangling yellow-green flowering bodies among the still garishly bright young foliage that had only just unfurled.

My ears were also filled with the songs of a score of feathered choristers. I could make out robins, blackbirds, thrushes, dunnocks, blackcaps, whitethroats, chiffchaffs, willow- and garden warblers. I went into the mews to move the hawks out onto their perches on the lawn, staining my bare knees green from the still bleeding grass. Then the familiar calls of a cuckoo broke out down the valley. I was filled with a warm glow – it was going to be a good day and this was indeed the embodiment of my childhood dreams.

Suddenly a chorus of chattering alarm calls broke out to one side. I walked carefully to the top of the lane to see the unmistakeable pied plumage of a pair of magpies a hundred yards down the drive. They were methodically working their way along the hedge, peering into the threadbare twigs, the leaves yet to unfurl fully. The raiders were cocking their heads and listening carefully as they went. Every now and then they would dive into the foliage like a cormorant on a lake, disappearing into twigs and leaves to re-emerge a few moments later with something in their beaks that was quickly wolfed down. The shrill calls of alarm and outrage now almost drowned out the dawn symphony. I ran down the lane, my dressing gown flapping, yelling angrily and the robbers flew off and this time it was they who were cackling in alarm.

I knew my intervention was only a temporary respite. The pillagers would return to work methodically along every other local hedgerow until the foliage grew too dense to have anything other than occasional success when they would turn to hunting worms and insects or scavenging road casualties and pecking for dropped scraps near the bins. Actually their raids don't have too much effect on the local songbirds because their breeding strategies revolve around two or three clutches each season. They try their hardest to fledge each brood, but the technique is designed to cater for at least one or two disasters.

It is not the same for most of the ground-nesters. They put everything into one large clutch and its loss spells a wasted year. As a result in many cases birds such as lapwings will form colonies. Just as a flock can provide protection in winter, be it from the benefit of scores of wary eyes as the birds feed or the confusion of swirling mist of individuals, so can a nesting colony provide protection for its members. Terns, for example, nest on shingle and turf along the coast and attract the unwanted attentions of predators such as foxes, black-backed gulls or skuas. When a raider arrives, the entire colony – including those from its most distant margins – will attack the interloper and can often drive it off with sheer weight of numbers. But this strategy depends on critical mass. Once the colony falls below a certain point, it can be the worst of all worlds. There are enough birds to attract unwelcome attention, yet not enough to intimidate the fox or gull.

When I first arrived there were six or seven pairs of lapwings near the cattle grid a quarter of a mile down the lane towards the main road. They would rise every time I drove past, flying on their instantly recognisable broad black and white bent wings as they whistled their 'pee whit' alarm calls. The next year they were down to four pairs and the following spring they appeared to have vanished. I found the remnants of the colony on the hilltop where three pairs were attempting to nest in the cover of clumps of marsh grass. It was a forlorn hope – if they couldn't survive in the warmer lusher pastures of the valley bottom, they had little hope out in the open of the mountain top. They were gone the next year and I haven't seen them since.

WELSH WEASELS

Birds might be easily the most visible local wildlife, but the mustelids, the weasel family have always been my favourite British mammals and I soon discovered Tan y Cefn has at least four resident species, with three the remaining three British species found within a few miles.

The smallest of the farm hunters is a particularly beautiful weasel that reared a family under the logs piled beneath the barn owl box. I would occasionally see her popping her head out of a hole near the water butt, two beady eyes mounted in a russet face. If I stayed very still, I might see her dash across the lane past the garage to the rear of the house. Weasels really can move! There would be a bouncing whisk of russet fur as she made the potentially dangerous crossing beneath the eyes and talons of the watching owls. Her destination was the rich hunting grounds outside the kitchen window. The rear lawn is held up with a series of buttresses made of railway sleepers disguised as flower and herb beds. Field and bank voles find the cavities and cover behind and beneath the sleepers irresistible. They build nests and secure runs here, safe in the knowledge that no kestrel, owl, polecat, stoat or fox can penetrate the fortress of timbers that took two burly men to manoeuvre into place.

But nature recognises no such thing as a truly secure hiding place. A weasel – particularly a female – is actually slimmer than a vole and can follow them anywhere. She is also a lot faster. In consequence I often watch her hunting up and down the sleepers as I wash the dishes. She is irresistibly active – constantly on the move, darting in and out of the gaps between the creosoted timbers to peer around for a few instants before slipping back into the labyrinth of hidden chambers.

Another lure for my lithe hunter is the constant possibility of catching an unwary dunnock or wren which are drawn to the area by the bird feeders hanging by the kitchen window. The more acrobatic species love to hang on the wire frames of the fat ball holders. In the depths of winter I can wash up while watching scores of assorted tits queuing in the bare stalks of last year's fennel. Colour comes from goldfinches with their bloody faces and black, saffron, white and olive plumage. They are far more garish than the gentle pinks of the linnets and the delicate flecked feathering of the greenfinches.

Many birds are choosy eaters as they cling to or perch on the feeders, but none more so than nuthatches which, with their thin black eye bands, are vaguely reminiscent of Zorro or the Lone Ranger. Unlike these champions of the disposed and bullied, they are anything but noble in behaviour, elbowing other waiting birds out of the way to get to the front of the queue. Then they hog the feeding aperture, flicking out dozens of seeds as they hunt for their grain of choice – although I have yet to understand what this might be. As a result the ground beneath the feeders is perpetually covered with various grains and suet particles. These are picked up by birds such as chaffinches, bramblings, reed buntings and dunnocks which prefer to scour the gravel beneath the window for scraps rather than hang clumsily on the feeders.

A feeding station like this is inevitably a lure for sparrowhawks, so the ground feeders are forever nervously flitting back to cover of the bay bushes and dense clumps of sage and rosemary in the sleeper beds. Here they may be safe from marauding hawks but risk running into the jaws of the quicksilver weasel.

The fallen seed naturally adds to the attraction of the area for voles and mice, but it is also a magnet for the rats which are an ever-present winter fact of farm life. I normally had a couple of tunnel traps below the bird feeders to catch a steady supply of the pests, but as soon as I saw the weasel flitting in and out of the sleepers I had to remove them. Bait is needed to trap most animals, but not the weasel family, all members of which seem magnetically drawn to the mysteries of a dark passage. Any drainpipe or slate leaned against a wall or three planks crudely nailed together is like a suspicious death to Poirot: they simply have to investigate. Thus my rat traps were far more likely to kill my beautiful russet hunter than the rightly hyper-suspicious rats that spend their nights scouring the ground beneath the feeders.

We also have stoats though I see them less often than their smaller cousins. Soon after our arrival I got up early on the summer solstice to soak up the atmosphere and walked down to the pond only to be brought up short by movement in the undergrowth on the other side. I paused and after a couple of minutes watching the mysteriously twitching wild garlic, was rewarded by four tumbling young stoats, falling out onto the shorter grass, in a cascade of writhing ruddy and white bodies with flailing black-tipped tails. For the next two or three days if I crept down to the pond and waited quietly I would be rewarded by the sight of these tumbling lithe youngsters. Sadly within a few days they disappeared, no doubt dispersing to set up their own territories.

It was a good decade later that I next spotted a stoat near the house. I was on the phone to a local naturalist on a frosty morning, making a cup of tea while looking out of the kitchen window, when my eye was caught by a movement in the over-vigorous patch of spearmint. Suddenly a stoat dashed out to run across the sleepers. Unlike the weasel he was too big to explore beneath the creosote-soaked beams. I flung down the phone and rushed to get my camera, although obviously by the time I returned it was too late. I was just in time to see him sitting bolt upright on his back legs like a Welsh meerkat to get a good view of his surroundings. A second later he was off again, tearing down towards the pond, long before I had time to focus let alone press the shutter.

The last time I caught sight of one was less pleasant. I was flying the goshawk beneath the badger sett and she landed in a mature sycamore a hundred yards away. Suddenly she plunged to ground and there was a brief jangle of bells. Clearly she had caught something which I assumed it was a squirrel caught away from the comparative safety of the boughs above. There they try to escape detection by clinging motionless to the far side of a branch – although few escape Sky's claws once she becomes aware of their presence. I walked briskly to the site and sure enough she was mantling, wings arched and shuffling around to keep her back to me as she glared back over her shoulder. This is always a sure sign she's caught something. I managed to manoeuvre in front and to my dismay saw the long curve of a brown body with a black-tipped tail.

My first instinct was to release the victim, hopefully relatively unhurt, if highly indignant, but no such luck. A moment later I saw her prey was missing a forelimb and was very definitely dead. Using a chicken wing 'tiring' (this is a tough bit of meat to engross the hawk), I extricated the corpse and slipped the stoat into my game pocket. There was a powerful and distinctly unpleasant musty odour. Most members of the weasel family have defensive scent glands which act as a natural mace (most famously in the case of the skunk).

The polecat is a slightly bigger member of the clan, and more common here than either of its smaller relatives. Its name is derived from the French *poule chat* or chicken cat. While they actually depend mainly on rabbits and voles, they are very real threat to poultry and ground-nesting game birds, so were ruthlessly persecuted by Victorian gamekeepers. By the First World War they had been exterminated from most of Britain, clinging on in parts of the Lake District, but with Mid Wales their unquestioned stronghold. They might be deemed the mammalian equivalent of the red kite and in common with the latter, they survived here largely because there was k little game preservation and they represented little real threat to farmers. While they would willingly kill poultry, polecats are nocturnal hunters and chickens are locked away at night. As a result polecats were welcomed on many farms as unpaid pest controllers, killing rats in the outbuildings and rabbits in the fields and hedgerows. So they survived in their Cambrian strongholds long after they had disappeared from the rest of Britain. All the same, as predators which relied heavily on rabbits, they were hit just as badly as buzzards when waves of myxomatosis swept across Britain in the second half of the last century.

They are undoubtedly more common than stoats or weasels around here, but are rarely seen because they are nocturnal. My best sighting was in mid-summer when bringing the children back from school. As I started up the side road to the house, I suddenly saw a small dark creature darting out of a drain in the middle of the road with the characteristic masked face of a polecat. The size clearly indicated a jill and she ran out of the metal grid, far quicker than any ferret I have ever owned. I stopped the car and watched as she suddenly realised my presence and darted back to disappear into the grill. I waited and, true to the weasel family's insatiable curiosity, her head popped back up a moment later, only to retreat before repeating the exercise.

Three years ago I had a memorable sighting while driving along the A40 near St Clears in Carmarthenshire. A female led her five kits across the road and the traffic in both directions came to a halt as the procession crossed. Apart from that, sightings of polecats in daylight are rare, but they are definitely still here. I find their characteristic three-inch long tarry black droppings on the hillsides and occasionally see one scuttling across the road in the headlights. But much more telling are the results from the trail cams which revealed regular visits from polecats to the pond, sometimes to drink, sometimes looking for rats or rabbits. And the frequency picks up in spring and summer when my two gill ferrets come on heat. If unmated they remain in this state, emitting a powerful hormone scent which is undetectable to the human nose, but which is irresistible to any wild hob within half a mile or so.

The farm's final resident weasel is the badger which is very definitely present in numbers. Our huge sett appears to be occupied for about six months to rear their young, but in early autumn the occupants decamp to another further up the hill. They are not difficult to spot with a powerful spotlight or caught in the headlights along local lanes at night, particularly in spring and autumn.

At one point, when peanuts were particularly cheap, I filled a couple of bird feeders with them. I was about to put the sack away, but then on a whim laid a trail of nuts from the field above down to the six huge windows which take up a large section of the rear wall of the barn conversion. After this it was merely a matter of scattering a few handfuls outside the windows and waiting for these to disappear overnight.

It didn't take long and once they were coming in every evening about an hour after dark, I positioned a floodlight to illuminate the peanut-strewn gravel. I would then pour myself a large mug of tea and sit quietly in the dark to watch them happily rummaging for titbits across the stone, only two or three yards away through the glass.

Unfortunately, badgers have their drawbacks. Most of the time they seem to live up to Kenneth Grahame's anthropomorphic Mr Brock: powerful, yet harmless – even avuncular – as they rummage around looking for slugs, worms and beetles. Yet they are still carnivores and will happily eat eggs, carrion and any mammal or ground nesting bird that they stumble across. Foxes are well known as serious and constant threats to poultry, but should they get a taste for chickens, badgers are arguably even worse. A fox can be deterred by the thin wood of a cheap hen house or even a strand of electric fencing. Neither of these will put off a determined badger and a couple of months after I started to put out the peanuts, the delightful visitors that I had lured to our windows discovered the easy pickings of the chicken run. First they were simply raiding the feeders, knocking over even the heaviest to spill the contents for easy eating. As the temperature dropped, however, they turned to the hen house itself and one night I lost four of my ten chickens in one hit.

It could have been a fox, but something told me it was a badger.

A few days later my suspicions were confirmed when I was late locking the 'girls' away. As I approached I heard the terrified squawks of a chicken in distress. I broke into a run and in the dim light of a small hand torch was confronted with the sight of a badger with a hen in its jaws. I was so close I could have kicked it. Indeed I drew back my foot to give it a hefty blow, but stopped as I remembered it has one of the strongest jaws of any British mammal. I left him to run off with my now silent chicken.

I shone the torch around the hen house through the pop-hole, but could see little except for feathers, some still floating. I locked it, but sadly the next morning my fears were confirmed. In the few minutes between dark and my arrival, the badger had clearly entered the hut and then, excited by the panicking birds, had gone into a feeding frenzy, biting and snapping and clawing until the flurry subsided. I had arrived just in time to see the last meeting its end. This incident and the inevitable growing winter rat issues meant I stopped putting out peanuts and the visits soon dried up.

There are three more mustelids to be found in the area, although I have only seen one of the three and that only on a handful of occasions, none of which were at home. Otters are shy and largely nocturnal. They too are another predator once almost wiped out across most of Britain, driven mainly by pollution to the under-populated uplands with their pure mountain waters. Otters rely heavily on eels for food and unfortunately these migratory fish build up various toxic organic chemicals in their fatty tissues. In a direct comparison to the DDT catastrophe with birds, these insoluble agricultural and industrial toxins would settle on the mud of a riverbed. Freshwater invertebrates such as water fleas and insect larvae sift through the silt and concentrate the chemicals. The eels gorge on the aquatic invertebrates and as long-lived fish which spend several years in freshwater, a large eel can contain a lot of toxins. As otters depend on an eel diet, they build up the toxins in their livers. This led to a dramatic decline in reproductive success and a population crash which saw otters virtually disappear from lowland England. Numbers remained relatively healthy in Scotland and the West Country, not to mention Mid-Wales with the Wye a particular stronghold.

My first sighting was unfortunately dead. It was a big dog otter killed on the main road near the Wye just south of Rhayader. I had just written an article about otters for one of the national newspaper and had spent a day with a conservation officer, Geoff Liles, who was charged with otter protection. We had driven around

Ceredigion inspecting riverbanks for spraints and fish scales, as well as visiting a small fishing lake whose slow-moving carp were being plundered by a nocturnal visitor.

As with my days out with Iolo Williams, the hours I spent in his company were deeply interesting. He explained no one knew how many otters there were in the Principality, mainly because their territories vary hugely in size according to the quality of the habitat – namely how many fish, particularly eels, there were to be had. In general, however, a long stretch of a major river would be patrolled by a dog otter whose main aim was to keep rivals away from the bitches that had smaller territories on its tributaries. The stronger the dog, the longer the stretch of river he could control, although no one was sure what this might be in Wales. In Scotland, however, a radio-tagged animal on the Spey dominated some seventy miles of this prime salmon fishery.

The best he could do was survey banks for traces of their presence in the form of spraints and footprints. The first are tarry fish-scaled droppings left every few hundred metres on minor landmarks such as rocks or partially submerged trunks to denote ownership of a territory. At the time they gave little indication of territory sizes, although DNA testing is now starting to change this.

'They're present along about eighty per cent of the Wye,' he said. 'That's the best in Wales.' He went on to explain that, unusually, while British otters had suffered a catastrophic crash in numbers during the 1970s, it was still one of their most important strongholds in Western Europe and the Welsh population was particularly important for the animals' long-term recovery.

'There are far more otters in Scotland, especially along the West Coast and in the Hebrides,' he said. 'But they are geographically isolated from the Lowlands and England by the industrial Central Belt.' Similarly although the West Country had a relatively healthy otter population, these were hampered in eastern movements by waterways which flowed north and south to the Bay of Biscay or Bristol Channel rather than east into southern England. In contrast Welsh animals found it far easier to recolonize the Midlands because there were so many watercourses running across the Marches and into England. Most notable among these were the Severn and Wye. Both rise in the heart of Wales and both had good otter numbers. And with dramatic improvements in water quality across the former industrial heartlands of the Midlands, the aquatic hunters are taking full advantage. They have already spread deep into England, even managing to climb the Cotswold escarpment and into the Thames catchment. There is still a dearth of science here, however, so when I saw the creature curled almost foetally on the roadside, I screeched to a halt and put it in the boot. Once home I measured it and found it was well over four feet from nose to tail-tip. Then I popped it into a bin bag and put it on top of the pizzas in the freezer for collection.

It was several years before I saw my first living otter – and I was surprised that this should be at the end of my lane, near the junction with the main road. It had clearly been drawn to the two large ponds created by a neighbour and stocked with a few rainbow trout and carp. Apparently they can scent fish droppings in the water and it would have followed the trail upstream to the source.

After that I caught one or two other glimpses of what I think were otters – V-shaped ripples moving up- or downstream as I crossed bridges the Wye or Elan, but nothing concrete. Then I had a magical experience as I left a pub in the Elan Valley late one night. As I got into the car I spotted what looked like a cat crossing the road, but somehow it didn't look quite right – very hump-backed and with too thick a tail. I sat quietly in the driver seat as it paused in the road and then ran towards me with a bumping gait. As it passed my suspicions were confirmed. It was a bitch otter, about the size of a large ferret and it was clearly set on a destination some way up the Valley. With a mixture of excitement and disbelief I followed her slowly up the road for 300 yards until she abruptly turned off towards the river.

The recovery of the otter is good news on more than one level. As its numbers declined, its alien relative, the American mink (which has also been spotted locally, although it is rare), has prospered on a national level. They started life here as an escapee from some ill-advised attempts at farm diversification between the wars. It rapidly proliferated along Britain's waterways and has decimated the water vole population: better known as Kenneth Grahame's 'Ratty'. Despite the fondness we have for the hero of *The Wind in the Willows*, they were generally ignored until someone noted their numbers were plummeting and blame was quickly pinned on the 'alien'.

Actually the mink boom was probably linked more to the otter decline than the presence of so many tasty bankside protein packages. Mink can certainly swim well and are more catholic in their diet than otters. They are far more inclined to take waterfowl and are easily small enough to venture down a water vole burrow, but in the end they are easily out-gunned by the bigger otter.

The good news however, is that the otters' spectacular come-back spells bad news for the mink. It seems they had previously flourished in what had effectively been a vacant, but rich, ecological niche of river and canal banks across much of Lowland England. The return of the otter to these lost hunting grounds means the mink are now in retreat. This natural competition has been helped in part because of an intensive trapping drive mounted not just by water bailiffs and gamekeepers, but by the far more powerful weight of the Environment Agency and Wildlife

Trusts. They use a cunning system which uses a floating platform supporting a tunnel containing a tray filled with damp clay. Many animals, but particularly mink, find the chance to explore the tunnel irresistible and as they run through, leaving their distinctive five-toed tracks behind. When these appear the tray can be replaced with a cage trap to allow undesirables to be removed without endangering our beloved otters and water voles. The result has been a crash in mink numbers and in some places at least, it seems vestigial vole populations have – if not recovered – at least managed to tread water.

The last weasel – and the one I would most like to tick off my 'seen' list – is the pine marten. As already mentioned, the native population may well still exist here, but it has certainly been boosted by releases near Devil's Bridge. These are gorgeous creatures which readily become comparatively tame. Across much of Europe they cause regular problems by raiding bins and taking up residence in attics. Book lovers will also recall Psipsia in *Captain Corelli's Mandolin* and to this day nature lovers can find them coming to treats in various car parks across the Highlands. I feel cautiously optimistic that the reintroductions will take off – and certainly the early signs are good.

HAWKS

The dire fortunes of farmland birds such as skylarks, curlews and tree sparrows have been well-publicised. Every year the press elegises over stories of disaster, outraged and panicked by the latest much-loved farmland bird to have experienced a catastrophic population crash over the past couple of decades. Yet at the same time, others quietly have been doing very well. Unfortunately, good news doesn't sell as well as negative, so the crises hitting corn buntings, skylarks or even starlings will always receive more page space than thriving species such as collared doves, natives that are thriving. The press still tends to focus on the negative side of more magpies or sparrowhawks. Many others, such as parakeets, Canada geese and ruddy ducks might also be in good shape, but their success is dismissed as 'invasive aliens'.

Nevertheless, some iconic, much-loved, natives are undoubtedly doing extremely well. Take the peregrine which is unquestionably the apex predator within its sphere and the fastest creature on earth. Certainly there are other birds – some ducks for example – which are faster in level flight, but in its favoured medium of a 'stoop', the peregrine is the fastest living creature. A cheetah can hit 60 mph going full tilt for a gazelle, but a peregrine easily exceeds 200 mph and some experts put it at over 250 mph when in wing-assisted free-fall. They are common in Mid Wales – to be seen almost everywhere. Indeed, by some measures this small area boasts the world's highest concentration of what is a genuinely global species with up to a dozen pairs within five miles of Rhayader. They nest on cliffs along the Wye and Elan Valleys and this is probably the main check on their numbers locally, for while most hills are steep, the number of real cliffs is limited. Indeed the pressure on nest sites means that the only record of a tree-nesting peregrine was made nearby in the 1980s when a bird ringer found a pair using an old raven's nest in a Scot's pine. This shortage of sites means a couple of regularly-used eyries are among what amount to little more than rocky outcrops and there is even one 'walk-in' nest among boulders on a very steep hillside. The farmer who owns the pasture once told me he'd visited this in late summer after the young had fledged to find it four inches deep in racing pigeon rings.

As predators at the very top of their particular food chain, peregrines have several hunting techniques: hard and fast level flight over fields or moorland, a long-ranging shallow attack from a clifftop vantage point, but most spectacular is the classic 'stoop'. This is mounted from altitude. The falcon uses wind and thermals to climb to hundreds or even thousands of feet above the ground. Once it has reached the required height, it hangs there lazily, barely beating its wings, but instead facing the prevailing air currents with outstretched wings to keep position as it scours the world below. It might be three to four hundred feet above the ground, but it could be five thousand, so high it is invisible to the human eye. This gives it dominion over a 'killing cone': an invisible shadow across the moorland or valley below which increases in size the higher the bird mounts. Thus the older and more experienced the falcon, the higher it goes. Should anything stray into the wind-thinned oval beneath, the hawk tips downwards and begins to fall, speeded by rapid wing beats to accelerate the descent. Within a few seconds it is hurtling towards the ground at over 200 mph.

The physics of this are staggering. At that speed no human could see anything, let alone chase evasive quarry, due to the sheer force of air against their pupils. They would also not be able to breathe properly, so would almost certainly pass out. Not, mind you, that they could get anywhere near that speed because their bodies are far too air-resistant. Spread-eagled skydivers reach terminal velocity around 120 mph – which is surprisingly slow if you think about it. Higher speeds can be achieved by head-diving towards earth, tucking in their limbs, but the stream-lined peregrine can effortlessly outstrip this. Indeed I've seen some wonderful footage of a parachutist leaping out of a hot air balloon above the Nevada Desert waving a lure. Ten seconds later a trained peregrine is released and within moments the bird has caught up with the man plummeting earthwards.

When I first sighted that peregrine with Iolo, she was directly above us and it was impossible to get an accurate idea of her size although she was clearly far larger and chunkier than a kestrel. I had stared up at this icon of everything I revered: a falcon! And by that I mean it in every sense that a falconer would understand. The word has many meanings. To an ornithologist it means a member of the Falco family – a pointed wing, speed specialist – which in Wales means a merlin, kestrel, hobby or peregrine. But oddly, it can mean more or less to a falconer. On the one hand, they might include regularly-flown non-indigenous species such as gyr, sakers or lanners, but a real purist would actually hone the term right down. A pedantic falconer would insist that a falcon can only be a female peregrine. Her mate is a tiercel – from the French 'tier' (a third) – because on average he is about one third smaller by weight than his partner. It is a perfect example of what zoologists would call 'reverse sexual dimorphism'. We anthropomorphic humans tend to think of creatures in mammalian terms with males bigger than females – the hulking dominance of a stronger male over his smaller mate.

It is also true among many birds with males usually larger and more gaudy than their mates. Here I picture cock pheasants, mallard drakes and cockerels. But when it comes to raptors the rules are over-turned. Females are often significantly bigger than their mates. At first this challenge to the apparent natural order causes most people to scratch their heads, but there are actually very good reasons for this.

Rapacious (active hunting) species have to defend a territory, particularly during the breeding season, and more importantly need to find enough food to rear their young. It makes sense for the pair to diversify. The best way to explain is to take the example of the pair of sparrowhawks that nest in a thicket behind the house. I love these feisty little hunters and always thrill to the sight of one flipping over the hedge in front of the car as I drive down a quiet lane, to fly rapidly barely a foot above the tarmac before flipping up and over the hedge in the hope of ambushing quarry on the other side.

These are not the most attractive of our raptors with their rather bulbous eyes and spindly frames, but they are fiery little hunters that will tackle birds far larger than themselves. In this they are very much the hawk equivalent of a weasel and have one of the biggest disparities in size between the sexes. The spar (female) is about the size of a dove, while her mate is not much bigger than a blackbird.

The pair begin courtship displays in late winter and by April the female is ready to lay and incubate. At this point her mate, a musket (from which the gun gets its name), is expected to supply almost all her dietary needs. He does this by preying on small birds, particularly exhausted migrants freshly arrived from Africa, cautiously placing his kills on a favourite plucking post near the nest. This is a wise move for he is so much smaller than her that his presence can trigger a hunting instinct in his hormonally charged mate akin to the famous risks to a male spider.

The eggs will hatch in early May and the female broods them for a week or two until they are large enough to keep themselves warm. By now their calorific demands are exploding so their mother abandons them to hunt as well. The musket continues to bring in small prey around the size of a finch, but the larger female can concentrate on bigger quarry ranging from blackbirds to pigeons. It's an ingenious strategy which means the pair needs a much smaller territory than were they the same size.

The same approach is followed by peregrines and goshawks. In both cases males are about a third smaller than their mates. This size diversity dwindles among other raptors and is barely noticeable among opportunist scavengers such as kites or buzzards. There is no benefit in a size distinction when your primary food source is already dead. The same goes for owls: there is no advantage in one sex being bigger than the other if you live exclusively on voles and mice. It is true that females tend to be very slightly larger, but the distinction isn't visible.

My fascination with birds of prey continued to develop over the first few years at the farm. One of the great benefits of the life of a freelance writer is that with a bit of imagination, I could get paid to follow my passion. The Elan Valley excursion with Iolo appeared in *The Independent*. This led to a *Country Living* commission which naturally required more research. It was during the last years of the twentieth century and we met in Llanidloes car park. For the rest of the day we tore around Mid-Wales. Iolo drives extremely fast and at the end of the day the imprint of my white-knuckled fingers were deeply embedded in his passenger seat.

Our first stop was a heronry in a pine plantation. Someone had reported hearing shots a few days before and Iolo wanted to follow this up. At first there seemed little to see, but as we picked our way around the wood, peering up, we made out the pale forms of birds draped over the upper branches. Some were adults, but most were pterodactyl-like fledglings still adorned with fluff. They had been blasted from their nests from below with a shotgun. Iolo suspected a local hotel which specialised in offering sewin (sea trout) fishing holidays to anglers was behind the crime, but clearly he could prove nothing. He said he would fire a warning shot across the owner's bow, but he doubted this would achieve much.

After this we went north to the Berwyn mountain range near Wrexham. These had once been managed grouse moors, but the area had long-since ceased to have enough game to be viable. Nevertheless the estates had pheasant shoots in the valley bottoms and the lowland keepers also kept an eye on the moors. Iolo explained he wanted to check on the local peregrines and hen harriers: 'They're here,' he said. 'But neither has fledged any young for at least a decade. It's obvious they're being persecuted and it's infuriating because it's totally pointless.' He explained that while he obviously decried all raptor persecution, in many cases he could at least see why it was done: 'If your job is all about rearing as many game birds as possible and you're judged by results, then you can see why they might want to get rid of goshawks or buzzards,' he explained wearily. 'But there is no shooting on these moors anymore – hasn't been since before the last war, yet persecution persists. It's a sort of visceral knee-jerk reaction among the keepers. They seem to think it will damage their reputation with their peers if they have hawks on their patch.'

As we trudged through the heather there was a sudden explosion and a large black bird hurtled into the air in a flurry of wing beats from the undergrowth in front of us before gliding down the hillside towards a young pine plantation. I just managed to catch a glimpse of its lyre-shaped tail. 'Remember that sight,' said

Iolo. 'You might not see one again – it's one of the last Welsh black grouse.'

This led to a conversation about the red kite reintroduction programme that had just been started with much fanfare in the Chilterns. A couple of dozen red kites from Spain were being released at a site in Oxfordshire whose precise location was being kept secret because of the threat from egg thieves. From the outset I found this attempt at mystery amusing because the 'top secret site' was near the giant cutting at Stokenchurch where the M40, one of the busiest roads in southern Britain, carves a huge gash through the soft chalk. Given kites are highly conspicuous, being large and addicted to soaring on thermals, the attempt at cloak and dagger secrecy was ludicrous. Any egg thief worth his salt would know exactly where to find the nests.

Iolo had his own thoughts on the reintroduction: 'I shouldn't criticise because it's my bosses who decided to do this,' he said. 'But it's bloody irritating. They've spent millions on this scheme and I can't really see the point. Welsh kites are doing very well at the moment and if the powers-that-be could just be patient the native birds would get to the Chilterns under their own steam. If I could have had just a fraction of the money they've spent on kites I might be able to save Wales's black grouse but they don't have the cachet of a red kite.'

Our conversation then turned to egg collecting. Iolo Williams said it was definitely still a problem, but it was dwindling because of the characteristics of the thieves. These were invariably men in middle or old age and their numbers were not being restocked by a younger generation. 'It's a strange hobby,' he mused. 'It's a sort of compulsive hoarding instinct. In some ways it's like train spotting – well, at least the enthusiasts are like train spotters. They are generally loners, some are married certainly, but they spend a lot of time on their own. In fact most of our successful prosecutions probably come from disgruntled ex-partners and wives.' Collectors rarely show off or boast about their treasures – not even to other enthusiasts – but instead hide them out of sight. In a late 1990s case some thirty-one thousand eggs were found hidden in a Midlands attic. No one had ever seen them: 'They just sneak off to look at the eggs and gloat in private,' said Iolo.

He went on to explain that it's not just about finding the nest of a rare bird and removing one egg. Instead they normally take the entire clutch (sometimes the nest as well). And finds are even more valued when there is something unusual about it – for example being in an unusual spot or containing more eggs than normal. Thus while peregrines might normally lay two or three eggs, on rare occasions they can lay as many as six. Likewise, while blue tits lay big clutches of around ten, occasionally they will carry on into the late teens. Most egg thieves would find both particularly exciting.

The aging profile of a typical egg collector means they are a dwindling band, but routine persecution is a much bigger problem. A couple of years beforehand a gamekeeper had told him he'd just found a goshawk nest with five eggs. In theory he would have needed a special licence to go anywhere near the nest, but Iolo let this pass. 'They won't fledge,' he sighed. 'In fact I doubt the nest is still there – but I won't be able to stop him.'

There were other motives for persecution. He told me of a family of pigeon fanciers in North Wales that would always raid the local peregrine eyrie. A couple of years before he had climbed up to check the clutch to find three eggs on which someone had written 'F★★k', 'You' and 'Iolo' in lipstick. He said that even though they were still in the scrape on the cliff ledge, they certainly wouldn't hatch – the climber had pricked each with a pin to kill the embryo, but had left the eggs to ensure the pair didn't lay another clutch.

Out on the moors the simplest way to do this for ground nesters such as harriers or merlins is to tip a chillbox of ice into the nest. Even if it's being watched, by the time anyone gets there the eggs will have been fatally chilled, but there's no evidence left. He said that although there was some persecution by game keepers, particularly in North Wales and egg collectors were always a worry, the biggest issues came with pigeon fanciers in South Wales. 'I know one peregrine eyrie near Merthyr which hasn't fledged a chick for fifteen years,' he said.

But the general picture for Welsh raptors has been almost universally good over the past quarter century. When Iolo took me on that first trip up the Elan Valley in 1994 there were eighty pairs of red kites in the Principality, concentrated along a forty mile stretch of the Cambrians. Since then numbers have exploded to over one thousand pairs. Their Mid-Wales heartlands are now saturated so they are having to overcome their natural reluctance to set up breeding territories more than five miles from their own natal nest. Fortunately there is still room for further expansion – they are still largely absent from much of Snowdonia and rare along the southern coastal strip. On the other hand they are moving east across the Marches and into Shropshire and Herefordshire. The population has been further swollen by a dozen of the introduction schemes that Iolo decried and as a result there are now several thousand pairs which have colonized huge swathes of the country.

Similarly other raptors, such as peregrines, experienced population crashes in the 1960s because of the pesticide DDT. Small birds ate the organo-chlorate-laden insects and these were eaten by sparrowhawks and peregrines. This concentrated chemicals which turned out to have egg-thinning qualities. Whole clutches would collapse under the weight of their incubating mother. As a result the populations of both dived (the number of breeding peregrines plummeted to barely three hundred in the early 1970s), but once the pesticides were banned, numbers began to recover sharply. At the moment there are eighteen hundred pairs of this cliff-nesting species in Britain: more than there have ever been since before the last ice age. This is thanks to a combination of a reduction in persecution and harvesting, but in the main due to the creation of manmade nest sites in the form of buildings and quarries across lowland England.

Buzzards have also done well after their numbers crashed during the 1950s due to the devastating impact of myxomatosis on the rabbit population. These big hawks rely on these during the breeding season, so the catastrophic collapse in Britain's rabbits meant buzzards had three decades of poor breeding success. As rabbits began to recover from the impact, so buzzards have recovered so much so that they are now our commonest raptor, with numbers going up five-fold from a low-point of about fifteen thousand to around seventy-nine thousand pairs today. This sizeable hawk has expanded out of its Celtic strongholds in Wales, Cornwall and Scotland to conquer the Midlands and even East Anglia. Similarly sparrowhawks have fared well since a post-DDT low point in the 1970s, doubling in numbers to around thirty-five thousand pairs today.

The good news has not been uniform, however. In the 1970s and 80s kestrels were our commonest raptor, but this was because their diet is mainly comprised of voles and mice which makes them less susceptible to DDT accumulations. They can and do catch small birds however, so while sparrowhawk numbers were depressed they undoubtedly took advantage of the vacated ecological niche by catching small birds which would normally have been predated by the more proficient sparrowhawks. More importantly perhaps, they benefited from the decline in buzzards, for this bigger raptor is a rival for the small rodents on which the kestrels rely. Once sparrowhawks and buzzards began to bounce back, the inflated numbers of kestrels declined, from the sixty thousand pairs of the 1980s to around forty-five thousand pairs today.

SPRING SKIES

From the outset I was struck by the incredible range of wild birds around my new Welsh home. There were plenty of birds in Oxfordshire, but the range was different and restricted. I could never identify more than a couple of dozen species. No sooner than I arrived in Wales I was amazed by the sight of birds I'd never spotted before. Most notable in the depths of that first very bleak, very wet, winter was a nuthatch. I was entranced by its blues, oranges and the wonderful black eye band which made it look like Errol Flynn playing a highwayman or Zorro.

Then I saw jays and great spotted woodpeckers at close range for the first time. Things really took off a few months later, just after the Easter birth of our son. Although the first migrants, chiffchaffs, had appeared a fortnight earlier, the main influx is in late April. Non-birders rarely notice the first signs. There is little to signal their arrival apart from a marginal increase in non-descript brown birds in the hedgerows. But after a while, the exhausted songsters which have flown some six thousand miles from Gambia and Senegal begin to sing and at about the same point the first most conspicuous migrants become visible.

The farmyard had always had one or two resident pied wagtails, but their numbers are swollen in spring by birds returning from the small-scale migrations to the coast. That spring they were joined by their flycatcher namesake. Warblers were probably the most challenging. Britain has about fifteen breeding species, almost all of which are migrants. Again, most are found in Mid-Wales, but identifying them is frustrating in the extreme. Almost all are drab brown/grey birds which like to skulk in undergrowth. There is almost no way to tell a willow warbler and chiffchaff apart, for example. Indeed the difficulty in identification is so great that it wasn't until the middle of the eighteenth century that Gilbert White discovered they were actually separate species.

The best way to tell everything apart is the song. These vary wildly, with many such as the blackcap, whitethroat, garden and willow warblers, having some of the most glorious calls of any songbird. Despite struggling to recall the songs, I persisted, doggedly listening to tapes and computer downloads, before rushing into the garden to listen to a particularly melodious chorister. I would then dash and listen again to the recordings on an ornithological website and try to correlate the two. It rarely worked – usually I couldn't click the two together and seemed unable to keep them in my mind, yet slowly I did manage to build up a repertoire to which I added sightings.

Not all the noise from the local birds could be described as song. From late winter the skies frequently ring with the cries of outraged crows, protesting at the presence of a buzzard. While the two certainly overlap when it comes to diet with both eating a fair amount of carrion, amphibians, worms and beetles, they don't openly compete for food and anyway scavengers tend to be less territorial than raptors. To some extent they benefit from the presence of others because by watching their movements they can learn about distant carcasses.

Nor is a buzzard a real threat to a crow – they are too slow to catch them in fair flight and disinclined to take on something that not only can fight back, but which is also likely to attract other crows to help in the scrap. As a result while the local skies almost always contain soaring buzzards and crows flying purposefully across the valley above or below, for most of the year the two species ignore each other.

The volume begins to rise in early spring, however, as suddenly the crows become aggressive towards the raptors and mercilessly dive bomb and harass them, usually in pairs, and all the while screaming out their irritation and obvious outrage. The dogfights carry on for the next three or four months, rising in volume and ire until mid-summer when suddenly the intensity drops off.

I noticed this but gave it very little thought for a few years. Then I stumbled across the answer while talking to Tony Cross, who runs the Welsh Red Kite Trust. He'd done some serious research into Shropshire buzzards. So often dismissed as 'lazy', this is a gross simplification. It is undoubtedly true that they might prefer to feed on small animals or carrion for much of the year, but this is actually very sensible. A physical fight risks damage to plumage, and breaking more than two or three primaries or tail feathers leaves the bird seriously handicapped – to an extent where it may well starve in bad weather. Thus it is hard to get even a trained buzzard to take a rabbit, despite having the benefit of a human to help quickly dispatch the quarry. I mentioned this to Iolo and he explained that while wild hawks may generally ignore rabbits, during the breeding season they have to up several gears.

'For most of the year the buzzards rely on small prey,' he explained. 'They do little more than fall on them and eat them on the spot. But when they have young they have to take food back to the nest. If they catch a vole and then fly a mile to give it to their young they've burnt more calories than they've delivered.' As a result when they have young the hawks must switch to bigger prey – possibly not adult rabbits, but certainly their half-grown young.

This same need for bigger protein packages also lies behind the crow's agitation. Buzzards might pose little threat to an adult crow – although I did once accidentally catch one in a catch 'em alive trap for magpies when it attacked the call bird – but they are adept at mugging young crows. They catch most by snatching them from the nest or pouncing on branches as they clumsily learn how to fly.

'If you go up to a buzzard nest after the young have fledged you'll find it's full of crow feathers and remains,' confirmed Iolo when I mentioned this to him. And it seems the same is true for red kites which also generally prefer small fare, but when a ringer came to for the two fledglings in the nest in the sycamore behind the house he remarked that the nest was full of the remains of grey squirrels and baby rabbits.

I was still a little sceptical that buzzards posed much threat to a young crow once it had left the nest, but one July my attention was caught by a cacophony from the hay field. There was a flurry out-raged caws from the surrounding trees and hedges, mainly from crows, but supplemented by the cackles of magpies and jays. I went to the gate, but at first could see nothing. Then I spotted two crows dive-bombing the long grass and briefly saw the raised wings of a large brown bird. I strode across the field, thistles and yellow rattle scratching my bare legs, to investigate. I was still some fifty yards away when the buzzard took off. I walked on to see what state its prey was in, but it was difficult to keep my eyes on the precise spot and at first I could find nothing, but then I saw a movement among the brown stems and saw a black form lying prostrate on its chest, surrounded by fluff and feathers. Its beak was open and it was gasping in terror and pain. Clearly the buzzard had started to pluck it alive when I arrived. I ran back to the house to fetch my camera but when I returned it had gone, leaving only a few wisps of white down amid the flattened grass.

The incident is an interesting reminder that a little field craft is much the best way of improving your wildlife sightings. In particular the mobbing of birds of all sizes reveals the presence of predators. In early summer the chattering of swallows is a good way of spotting the elusive sparrowhawk. Look up and they will be swooping around the long-tailed little hunter, knowing they are safe provided they know where it is. Closer to the house, the ticking alarm calls of a wren tells me when the barn owls are hunting by daylight.

Falconers have harnessed this behaviour for centuries to find lost hawks that have disappeared in hot pursuit of quarry. If they kill or find a good vantage point from which to look for fresh prey, they can freeze over their prize or simply sit motionless on a branch. In this case the leg and tail bells which, until the recent invention of telemetry, were the best way of finding a hawk could be silent for long periods. Fortunately, when this happens, more often than not other birds will spot it and set off alarm calls – particularly when it has taken one of their number. Magpies and jays are especially sensitive to their presence and their calls have the volume to carry a fair distance.

But back to spring birdsong: even the most confirmed town dweller instantly recognises the call of the cuckoo. In late April each year the familiar calls of the males ring out across local fields as they announce their territories to the more demure females (whose bubbling calls sound much more like those of a curlew). They have been experiencing sharp declines across most of Britain, but remain relatively common in Mid-Wales. Numbers vary, but there are usually at least three males calling within earshot of the front door.

These are fascinating birds. Although insectivorous by diet, they are a serious threat to two or three local songbirds because their ingenious reproductive strategy relies on a form of predation. These brood parasites are one of the wonders of the natural world. Most people know they lay their eggs in other birds' nests and that when the changeling hatches it evicts the nest's rightful occupants to usurp their home and devour the food which should be rightly theirs. Understandably this has culturally been treated with distaste. 'You're a cuckoo in the nest,' is a phrase of revulsion. The youngster is the ultimate epitome in treachery: a fosterling who betrays the hospitality of well-meaning and devoted parents by killing his foster siblings and greedily gobbling up their birth right.

Actually the whole process, if a bit macabre, is one of the wonders of the Welsh countryside. This bird defies so many natural rules. To start with the cuckoo's eggs. While males come in a standard genetic package, there are at least five strains of female, each literally a specialist. This is because like most birds there are pigment organs in her oviduct which give her eggs a distinctive pattern. For most birds these are purely for camouflage or as pro-tection against parasites such as cuckoos – a strange-looking egg in the nest spells danger.

In a natural arms race, female cuckoos have evolved to mimic their hosts. Thus some females produce eggs which resemble those of a dunnock while others lay eggs coloured like those of a reed warbler. In my area the unfortunate victims are usually meadow pipits, for the familiar calls of the males generally come from a conifer plantation above the house which overlooks open hillside which has a healthy pipit population. This is only too evident on my weekly walks to the cairn which overlooks Rhayader. Their drab brown forms flit from the gorse and bracken in front, issuing their piping alarm calls.

The female cuckoo will therefore patrol her territory, keeping out a beady eye for pipits to the exclusion of other ground-nesters such as skylarks or wheatears. When she spots activity, she calls lustily. When one of the two or three resident males respond, they mate. She may still have semen from a previous mating inside her – it can stay viable for up to a fortnight – but whatever happens, a day or two later she slips in furtively to the pippet nest to lay an egg in the grass-lined nest beneath the gorse or bracken.

If she is lucky, the hosts will fail to spot both the raid and the presence of another, similarly-patterned, large egg. But the intended victims of this crime are not as helpless as one might imagine and more often than not they do realise something is amiss and abandon the nest to start afresh elsewhere. When things go the cuckoo's way, her egg has a speeded-up incubation period of just twelve days, which means it should hatch first.

They are amazing in so many other ways too. The really big question is how does a cuckoo know it's a cuckoo? All other birds are reared by parents, usually in the presence of siblings. This gives them the chance to learn all about what they are through the imprinting process. Their parents' appearance tells them what an ideal mate should look like, while they learn to socialise with others of their species from their siblings. Yet a cuckoo is denied these lessons.

But that's not the end of the story. The young cuckoo will have been fed a diet of caterpillars, insects and worms, but it will never have eaten the hairy larvae of the bombycid moths. These are toxic for most birds, so their foster parents will not have brought these to the nest. Cuckoos have a renewable stomach lining which coats the spines and protects them from ill-effects. How the young birds discover this for themselves is a mystery, but they do soon after leaving the nest. This gives them a competition-free source of food for the demanding migration ahead – but this only leads to another wonder – how the cuckoos know where to go? Many migrants such as swallows fly south in company, presumably following the lead of an older bird. Cuckoos travel solo, relying entirely on instincts buried deep within their DNA.

Recent satellite-tagging has shown the males follow one of two main routes to their wintering grounds in Senegal, Gambia and the Congo. The shortest is through Spain and across the western Sahara, while the alternative is down Italy and due south across and the Sahara to the Congo Basin. Surprisingly, David, a Welsh male tagged near Tregaron in 2016, chose the Italian route, while birds from East Anglia seem to prefer the Spanish flight path. It seems David was shrewd, for while this route involves crossing the desert at its widest point, eastern migrants tend to fare better, probably because there is more food in the lusher valleys of Northern Italy than in Spain, so the birds stock up on vital calories before beginning the dangerous two thousand mile desert crossing.

Perhaps the most incredible aspect of all, however, is how the birds behave when they return to Wales next summer. They touch down in an area near the site where they hatched and after a day or so begin to call. They hear a strange reply – a song they will have never heard before – and instantly recognise this as belonging to a suitable mate.

Despite their familiar song cuckoos are surprisingly difficult to spot. They are grey, pigeon-sized, birds which in flight look remarkably like a sparrowhawk. Whether this resemblance to a hawk prompts alarm in songbirds or whether they instinctively recognise the parasite, they are relentlessly mobbed and these shrieks often are as good an indication of a cuckoo's presence as its call. Indeed, until comparatively recently it was commonly believed that at the end of the breeding season they mutated to spend the bulk of the year as sparrowhawks.

Although I know what to look for and in late spring we have at least two or three calling males nearby, I only spot them a couple of times each summer – and the window is remarkably short. In a normal year I hear the first in the last week of April and the final call comes barely two months later, making this one of our most fleeting visitors. This makes sense: all the other migrants that are drawn to our shores in summer need not only to set up territories, mate and lay, but to incubate and rear – and the last two easily take two or three times as long as the territorial and mating processes.

The brevity of the stay is celebrated in a traditional rhyme:

The Cuckoo comes in April
She sings her song in May
She changes her tune
In the month of June
And in July she flies away

While cuckoos might generally be furtive and difficult to spot, this doesn't mean they can never be seen. One of my most remarkable wildlife sights came on a June afternoon. We'd had guests for Sunday lunch and just before they left I spotted two birds sparring with each other as they flew in tightening concentric spirals above the front lawn, climbing higher and higher as they chattered angrily at each other. I was mesmerised, staring at the pair as each concentrated on daunting their opponent into retreat. At first I couldn't work out why two sparrowhawks would act like this, but then realized they were a pair of male cuckoos, presumably tussling for territory. The sight is etched on my memory even now, a quarter of a century later, I have certainly never witnessed anything comparable since and any cuckoo sighting is a comparative rarity.

A simple egg, by the way, is fascinating for all sorts of reasons. From an engineering perspective it is just brilliant: strong from the outside yet very weak from within. In other words, its curved surface resists external pressures well, distributing forces in the same way that an arch takes the weight of the wall above. Yet when it has very little ability to withstand internal pressures – the chick locked inside finds it comparatively easy to tap its way out using the little tooth on the end of its beak as a chisel.

The shell is miraculous in other ways too. It is porous, allowing air in and carbon dioxide out – and to a limited extent moisture can also flow in both directions. To help all this, there are also two thin membranes on the inner side of the shell. These keep the developing chick from becoming deformed by sticking to the shell. The membranes can also stick to the shell as moisture slowly evaporates from the albumen, so the egg needs to be regularly turned to keep things lubricated and free moving. The parents naturally do this each time they return to the nest and will also stand and roll them with their beaks before settling back down again.

The clutch has its own quirks too. As already mentioned, all birds lay uniquely coloured and shaped eggs – which is what attracts the collectors – but scientists are still less than certain about the true reasons. There are a lot of theories. For many years it was thought the shape of the egg was linked to the structure of the nest. Birds which have cupped or at least enclosed nests tend to have relatively rounded eggs. It was thought this was because they were easier to turn and the cupped nest meant there was no risk of the precious cargo rolling out. On the other hand cliff and ledge-nesting species generally have very oval or even pointed eggs. This was thought to reduce the risk of rolling off the rocks, but it's now believed the shape of auk eggs, for example, is actually linked more to their body shape. Guillemots, for example, lay just one very long, pointed egg, on their guano-covered sloping cliff nests. This is twice the weight of a similarly-sized chicken which lays far larger clutches of around a dozen. The auks put more nutritional reserves into their single huge egg in order to speed up the chick's development on its perilous cliff nursery. The shape was thought to have evolved to reduce the risk of losses because the eggs naturally tend to roll in tight circles. Now the scientists have changed their minds and decided these disproportionately large eggs need to be shaped this way precisely because they barely roll at all – not because they might fall off, but to save space.

The birds choose to nest in crowded elevated cliff colonies for mutual protection. This means they have very little space or choice in the slope of their nest ledge. The egg is always vulnerable, but never more so than at the vital changeover point when their parents swap incubating duties. So as the adults shuffle carefully over the precious egg, this remains almost motionless on the steeply sloped, narrow rock ledge. This same risky moment would spell disaster for a more conventionally-shaped egg – such as those of their relatives the razorbills which prefer earthy hollows between the rocks.

Colour is another factor which varies wildly between species. In many cases camouflage is clearly important. Ground-nesting birds such as waders generally have brown and black flecks on a sandy-shaded shell. These blend into the beaches and bogs where they nest to become almost invisible from a distance of only a few inches. The need for markings on eggs laid in cup-shaped nests is more difficult to understand. After all, if a predator has found the nest, they have also found its contents. One theory is that the pigments can provide additional strength to the calcium carbonate of the shell. Another is that it is partial protection from brood parasite cuckoos which have to specialise on one prey species by laying similarly coloured eggs. Those of a barn owl are relatively small and unremarkable in appearance. They closely resemble a table tennis ball – white and almost spherical. This is good for turning and fitting several into a relatively small and confined space.

By late June the owlets were growing exponentially. Their mother had brooded them for the first week or so, but then started to leave to hunt, returning to delicately pop morsels of meat into the hungry beaks. She would then brood them again, but with decreasing enthusiasm. After three weeks she left the box to perch nearby – either on top of the chamber or in the roof of the garage on the other side of the lane.

This doesn't mean she was neglectful, far from it, for she was now seriously pestering me, swooping across the lane to snatch chicks from my outstretched palm. At first she restricted these flights to the hours of darkness, appearing suddenly as a ghostly form at the window or to land on the water butt by the front door.

As soon as I opened the door she would fly at me, expecting food. If I was slow to proffer my hand with its chick garnish, she would land on my arm or head, hissing in indignation. And when she did take the food, she invariably grabbed it in her beak, before almost immediately wheeling off towards the nest. For no apparent reason her route back to the nest would vary between window, door or wheeling around the back of the building to swoop in through the large opening which had once been sealed by double barn doors. As she flew she would deftly move a foot up to seize the chick from her beak and it would be dangling beneath her as she entered the barn.

As her brood grew and their demands increased, she became more active by day and would come immediately whenever I called, but she was notably shy when other humans were present. That said, she would still delight the visitors by flying around the garden, swooping in close to my offering before thinking twice of it.

When it came to my resident owls, by the end of June even the male was often in evidence. By now the owlets had prodigious appetites and it was proving hard for their parents to sate their constant demands while nights were barely five hours long. This drove the adults to hunt by day. They were most evident just after dawn and in the evening twilight, but even in broad daylight the outraged twittering of the swallows or martins would alert me to the male flying over the lawn to hunt in the hay meadow in broad daylight.

Owls are known for being silent, but they can also be very noisy, particularly when perched in the seclusion of the barn or garage. They may hunt by floating back and forth over fields without a sound to pounce on their unsuspecting victims, but back near the nest they have a wide range of calls. Everyone is familiar with the 'too-wit, too-woo' territorial calls of the tawny owl, but in comparison with these aggressive and generally solitary woodland hunters, barn owls are far more sociable.

As a result they have many calls to indicate a wide range of emotions: everything from fear, hunger, marking out territories, discovering suitable nest sites, invitations to mate and aggression. In contrast to the relatively melodious calls of the tawny, these are anything but tuneful. Instead barn owls vocalise with shrieks, hisses and snores and beak snapping.

Indeed they are so vocal ornithologists monitor them by quietly visiting suitable buildings and hollow trees in spring and summer. As I have said, for a fairly large white bird, they are surprisingly difficult to see, so instead it is much more reliable to listen intently for the territorial shrieks of the adults or the hisses of the young in the nest. This is certainly how I first became aware our first pair were breeding. I was charging out to mow the lawn when I became aware of strange snoring sounds from the nest box in the eaves.

Ironically, their vocal habits are thought to be partially responsible for their decline over the past half century. Studies suggest virtually none are found within half a mile of any major road. Many fall victim to collisions, for unlike the up/down hunting technique of the kestrel, quartering across motorway verges a few feet off the ground is asking for trouble. But the vehicle noise pollution is just as damaging, drowning out vital communication with mates and rivals.

By the middle of July the oldest owlet was almost ready to leave the nest. It was almost fully feathered, with bits of fluff hanging to the top of its head, while the youngest was still half-quilled. All of them were exercising by energetically flapping their wings above their backs. The youngest was still far from striking, but certainly much more appealing than they had been during their first two or three weeks when the near bald chicks sported huge beaks out of all proportion to their tiny frames. Two weeks later they had all left the box, driven out in part by the appalling smell of guano and rotting meat. For a few days they could be seen perching uncomfortably on beams, branches or the children's climbing frame as they were dive-bombed by the swallows and house martins.

Although barn owls can theoretically breed at almost any time of year and multiple clutches are common, for the past couple of years my pair's parenting is over by August. The male is nowhere in evidence, but the females begs just as insistently for food although she is reverting to her normal nocturnal habits. Normally she would make her feelings clear simply by landing on the feeding station outside the window. Over time, however, she learned first to land on the window sill behind my computer where she would sit until I went out with a chick. Later she discovered the kitchen was the house's focal point where one of its windows was once a 'pitch hole'.

All the other windows are mounted almost flush with the outer wall, but this was once just a two foot square gap through which hay was thrown to feed the cows in what was once a dairy. It is now simply a glazed pane set against the inner side of the two foot thick wall, with a large slate sill in front. This means it is sheltered even in a storm and she can sit there, hissing quietly, until she's noticed and someone goes out with food. She would fly straight in to land lightly on my hand for a moment and pick up the morsel in her beak before flying off towards the cover of the barn opposite, deftly transferring it to her foot in mid-air.

This isn't to say she is entirely friendly. She is not averse to clipping me over the head when hungry. As I go out to feed her, she screams and hisses, telling me she's famished and rebuking me for being tardy with her food. She then flies at me, usually banking off at the last minute – but not always. Sometimes she will clip me, catching her claw across the top of my head as she flies off to a perch on the other side of the yard. It doesn't draw blood or hurt, but is always an unpleasant surprise, particularly because it often comes completely out of the blue. As a silent hunter, unless you see her coming the first you know is when you receive the blow.

Barn owls are much less territorial than tawnies. Indeed provided there is enough food, they are quite prepared to nest extremely close to each other. A bird ringer once told me he'd had two occupied boxes in the same farmyard. My neighbours, only four hundred yards down the lane also say they regularly see a barn owl going in and out of one of their outbuildings. That's close enough to be one of my birds, but I would guess it's another pair, although this is difficult to gauge. It depends on territories – or to be precise what they contain in terms of protein packages (which effectively means voles). A healthy owl probably needs about three small rodents a day and of course that multiplies several times over if it is to rear a brood. Most local fields are over-grazed, the grass nibbled virtually down to the roots by Iolo Williams' 'woolly maggots'. This deprives the voles of both food and cover and they are virtually absent from huge swathes of the countryside. I have always taken a far more ecological approach to my thirteen acres and these are only lightly browsed by cattle and sheep over the spring and summer, leaving the ground covered with tussocks and seed-bearing weeds. This would appear to suit the owls because in spring and summer they appear to head out to my badger field and hay meadow to do the bulk of their hunting. The neighbours who are so anxious to attract owls of their own adopt a similar approach to land management, to the mild disgust of the two neighbouring farmers who feel a more intensive grazing approach would be far more efficient. And of course, however good the hunting, the owls have to share the available voles with diurnal hunters such as kites and buzzards, weasels and stoats – plus the plentiful tawny owls patrolling the hedges and woodland edges. The result is that I suspect the fields within a few hundred metre radius or so could only support a couple of pairs of barn owls at most

WEATHER

People in towns grumble about lack of daylight in winter, but they don't know what they are talking about. In December and January the sun rises after 8am and sets soon after 4pm giving only eight or nine hours of natural light. Urbanites are obviously aware of this, but their lives are cushioned by tungsten and florescence. One walks from office to street-lit pavement, warm shops, cafés and restaurants, bright buses and trains and the cosy warmth of home. Most of these are lacking in the countryside. It is an over-riding feature in the country and ever more so the further west and north one travels. In winter it seems as if one gets up in the dark and yet almost as soon as one is dressed it's night again. In winter I genuinely can't see any lights after 5pm if I look out of the front windows – none.

But there is a reverse side to this coin. Days get longer remarkably quickly after the winter solstice. As early as New Year one is aware that the sun is coming back and within a few weeks days are lengthening by several minutes every day. By Easter each is five minutes longer than the last – that's an extra hour each fortnight – and in high summer it is light around 4.30am and it isn't dark until after 10pm. In late June I can watch the hard-working owl parents fly urgently across the lawn towards the hay meadow to return a few minutes later dangling a small brown package. A fortnight later the young owls have emerged to perch on the climbing frame while outraged swallows dive-bomb them until it becomes too murky to see.

These are the lazy days when I can have no doubts about the joys of living here. In good weather outdoor tasks such as gardening or cleaning out an animal's pen cease to be chores and instead become welcome distractions. When a visitor pops in for a cuppa or glass, then what could be more natural than sitting on the deck with the Brecon Beacons in the background and willow warblers trilling around the pond? But all seasons have their appeal. Autumn conditions are often – nay, usually – better than high summer, with warm, cloudless, days. The clear skies lead to cool nights which in turn produce 'inversions' when the cold damp air drops to the valley bottoms which fill with mist, but leave the hill tops poking out.

I am frequently above the clouds, thanks to the farm's height. In the morning it can be like looking across a white sea to the surrounding hills protruding from the formless blanket-like islands. This is a mixture of monochrome and colour, for the black and white mist-swathed valley is topped by deep blue skies with pure white clouds, enriched even more at dawn by the yellows and oranges of the rising sun.

I once spent a year in Australia and although I loved the people, the landscape and wildlife, there was a nagging sense of disconnection. Wonderful as it all was, something just wasn't quite right. And then I realised it was because the seasons were so much less pronounced than back home. Over there winter morphed apparently seamlessly into spring which then slid into summer.

Welsh weather is far more strident. One moment it's summer and the next it's autumn – or at least you have a clear blast of what's to come. A couple of days later the temperature may pick up again, but regardless of the mercury you always know the time of year and it's all down to colour. The garish yellows, oranges, reds and russets of autumn change to the blacks of bare damp twigs and the limp greens of barely-growing grass. Even the last then fades over winter until everything seems to be muted. The grass is faded to the most washed out of greens, yellows and browns that clearly announce all the nutrition is exhausted.

And then, just when the landscape seems as dead as it could possibly be, around Easter suddenly everything changes. One moment the grass is listless and drained of life: the next the fields have turned a deep vibrant green and garish young leaves are breaking out along the hedgerows and tinting the browns and blacks of the skeletons of oak woodland.

This still leaves autumn as the most striking season, even if it varies from year to year, dependent on late summer weather. In a good year the Elan and Ystwyth Valleys can put on a display to rival New England: the hillsides cloaked with a vibrant mix of green, yellow, orange-brown and red. The intensity of the pallet depends on summer growing conditions coupled with the speed at which the temperature dips. A healthy leaf gets its green colour from the vital chlorophyll with which it turns sunlight, air and water to make sugars. The plant continually refreshes the pigment through the spring and summer, but as the days shorten and the nights get colder, the renewal process slows and the leaves begin to adopt various tones of yellow, orange and brown.

Some of the most striking colours, the reds, come from the reaction of sunlight on the increased sugar levels inside the plant. An obvious example is the red hue on apples – particularly on the side facing the sun – but it also occurs in the leaves of various sweet-sapped trees such as maples, sycamores and beech. The intensity of colour depends on weather: sunny days followed by chilly nights produce deeper reds, for example. Calm weather is also important, for high winds and lashing rain will strip the leaves from the branches overnight, while a placid autumn can see foliage hang on well into November.

The colours are not confined to leaves, but are supplemented by the vibrant seasonal berries, fruit and fungi. Along the hedge bottoms fly agaric, the classic red and white spotted toadstool, burst forth, while above them scarlet rosehips and spindle berries add a dash of colour to the thinning hedges. Set against these are sour sloes, covered with a yeast bloom of Prussian blue and bitter beyond belief. Clusters of garish red rowan berries hang above the lanes and although the holly berries are yet to achieve their seasonal Christmas reds, by now they are clustered yellow among the glossy leaves. Voles and squirrels clamber the briars and hazel to feast on the last blackberries and browning cobs alongside the whispy white strands of 'Old Man's Beard'.

As the nights draw in and the mercury begins to drop, heat becomes an increasing preoccupation. When we arrived the place had three night store heaters, but we were otherwise reliant on the wood burner in the living room. This was a large cast iron stove with a back boiler, we arrived in one of the wettest winters on record and we had no fuel. This went down badly with my pregnant partner and thus ever since I have had been mildly obsessed with laying down sufficient dry wood to keep us through the colder months. This preoccupation builds up over the year and I am always convinced that this year I have got enough, only to inevitably decide in February that I have misjudged yet again.

I liked the idea of heating the house the traditional way. And there was something implicitly self-sufficient in harnessing local trees instead of a fossil fuel for heat. It seemed splendidly romantic. So what if the fire didn't lift the ambient temperature quite up to normal central heating levels? Nothing wrong with putting on an extra layer or wearing a woolly hat indoors!

Over time I became far more adept at creating heat from wood. Seasoning is the key – something which most modern Britons seem incapable of grasping. My cousin Hugh, a free-wheeling ex-potter; hedger; musician; forester; radio producer and building-restorer, has lived for the past four decades in houses next to rivers, most recently on the Shropshire border and now near Brecon. He is anally obsessive about the need to have two years' fuel stacked and drying at all times. Now although I share his point, here he is in a league of his own, spending much of his spare time neatly-stacking shed upon shed with perfectly cut and split faggots.

That said, we share a pride in our green credentials on this issue. We have each heated our houses almost entirely with wood for many years. This means twenty-five years in my case – more like fifty for Hugh. The whole process of felling, cutting, storing and splitting wood slowly becomes an increasing priority. We both probably started mainly through parsimony (wood is a lot cheaper than any alternative), but about twenty years ago we found that out of the blue the global media were wheeling behind us. I could show off my machismo and eco-friendliness by showing city friends my wood piles, chainsaw and axe. Certainly the house might be slightly on the cool side by urban standards, but to my mind not significantly so.

There are many other invisible benefits that come with a reliance on wood for heat. Perhaps the most important are that it is yet another tie to the natural world. One winter shivering in front of a cold stove burning wet wood teaches important lessons about trees, weather, seasons, forward planning and seizing the day. It is a strong drive to get one to look at and bond with one's surroundings, starting with noting dead or dying trees and their species. If these are on a neighbour's ground, then a sly approach over a pint may yield dividends.

Next comes an awareness of weather. This is most obviously vital in winter when it comes to checking how much fuel is going to be needed that evening, but storms can produce a future fuel bonanza. It also teaches the discipline of being acutely aware of sunset: stumbling around a woodshed in the dark leads to bruised shins, twisted ankles and bad language.

Although dwindling daylight, rain and cold shut down outdoor life for most humans and there are far fewer bird calls, this doesn't mean wildlife has gone into cold storage. Increasingly large flocks are assembling, gathering together for the security of numbers. There are various factors behind this, the first is that with food in short supply, the birds are having to venture further and further from the relative safety of the cover of woods and hedgerows.

With the skies patrolled by falcons and harriers while hawks, foxes and weasels stalk the hedgerows, this is a serious risk. Some, such as the peregrine, generally hunt from above, scouring the ground below from a clifftop perch or effortlessly surfing the winds and thermals while looking for the weak or inattentive. Masters of the invisible air currents, far from being buffeted into submission by high winds, these jet fighters of the bird world revel in storms, knowing their prey is distracted as it battles the conditions. Few birds are as comfortable in near hurricanes as a peregrine. Instead they struggle to reach cover or find food, taking their eyes off the threat from above. This tilts the perpetual delicate see-saw between predator and prey in favour of the former.

This is not the only threat. Hedgerows are stalked by weasels, stoats and foxes, while goshawks and sparrowhawks are speed merchants, attacking fast and low along their borders, flicking up and over the tangled briars and thorn to catch quarry in the fields some yards away from its cover. Or they come in beneath the radar, mounting low-flying gliding raids where their brown or grey forms are almost invisible against the broken background of lifeless shrubs and dead bracken.

In times of relative plenty, healthy birds are fairly safe. They are wary and ever-alert to danger and they know that provided they stay in close proximity to trees or hedges they can get to the safety of cover, negating the hawk's advantages of speed and agility. In winter the shortage of food and light means many birds are forced further and further into the open. They also have to work harder to find what little food there is, reducing their ability to check constantly for danger. How can a starling both probe the turf for leatherjackets while keeping an eye on the skies above and the tangled shrubs and dying bracken bordering their foraging grounds?

The answer is to resort to the protection of numbers. Lots of birds mean many eyes provide an ultra-sensitive early warning system. Thus while the flock of starlings or lapwings pick their way across the open ground, scouring the soil or turf for worms and insect larvae, there are always sentinels looking for danger. And when it arrives in the form of peregrine or sparrowhawk, the entire flock lifts as one – or rather not as one, but as a swirling, moving cloud of individuals. The hawk is faced by a mystifying eddying torrent of wings and feathers that clatter up in front of them, a clattering, jabbering swirl of colours and shapes.

All the same, the threats facing any prey build up. As the weather worsens, so calories and shelter are in ever shorter supply. To make matters worse, the days are shrinking and soon all creatures are chasing their tails to gather the food they need to survive. As a result by December even comparatively large and non-social birds look to the safety of numbers. Flocks of pigeons, starlings, thrushes, and mixed groups of crows, rooks and jackdaws look to each other for security. During most of the day the tussle between predator and prey is fairly straightforward – the birds feeding in the fields rely on communal observation to take to the wing and then to cover before it is too late. Life becomes more risky when they start to roost for the night. They are all too aware that the hostile eyes keeping them under constant surveillance know the sheltered cover to which they are certain to return.

Here the raptors are akin to nature's U-boats patrolling the Atlantic to starve the British into submission. They know their prey's movements are ultimately predictable and where to wait to pick off quarry. The German submarines would lurk in the sea passages which merchant vessels would have to use and initially were devastatingly successful. Back in the war, the response was safety in numbers and sailing by zig-zagging rather than taking a straight line.

The local flocks have evolved similar strategies. They grow increasingly noisy to disrupt the predator picking up on signs of weakness. As they reach the potentially very vulnerable point of landing at the roost, they swirl around and above the roost in the conifer plantation above the house, hundreds of pairs of eyes scouring for a lurking goshawk in the upper branches and the skies above. To fly in alone would be asking to be picked off by the peregrine circling high above, or ambushed by the hawk.

Thus in early December the jackdaws, crows and rooks that have been feeding in small groups across the local fields begin to group together in the open as dusk approaches. One family group joins up with another and then another. After a while they take off, calling loudly to each other and flying back in the vague direction of the roost, swirling and wheeling as they go. This behaviour acts as a magnet to other groups and slowly the flock builds in size, not just on the individual night, but over the coming weeks. Before Christmas the group will be just twenty or thirty strong, but by late February the flock numbers several hundred and is very noisy indeed.

Winter bird activity is not just about survival. I used to think the breeding season was a spring phenomenon, but for many creatures the concept seems to lurk as a constant background urge.

Even in the depths of winter there are signs of what's to come. Mistle thrushes start to gang up towards the end of August in family groups which later join together to form small flocks. They give off their instantly recognisable football rattle calls as they bounce through the air above the fields, but by the end of the year these groups have disbanded. Instead of looking for the security of a flock to evade predators, the males are beginning to get a head start on next year's breeding season. They do this by searching for a berry-laden food source. Indeed, the bird's name comes from its fondness for mistletoe, that strange shrub, a living green sphere that hangs in bunches from the apparently lifeless limbs of oaks and apple trees. A glance at its fleshy white berries and strange green leaves and it isn't difficult to see why the druids apparently venerated it as a sign of life in the depths of winter. The oak or crab apple host would be no more than a black skeleton, yet its passenger would appear the embodiment of life. Mistletoe is rare in Radnorshire, although it is common enough a few miles away in the acres of Herefordshire cider orchards.

My mistle thrushes are drawn mainly by the lure of another tree beloved by pagans and one which is, if anything, even more associated with Christmas. There is a particularly splendid and always well-endowed holly halfway down the lane. The berries grow slowly all autumn, green and hard and invisible among the glossy spiked leaves until they burst into view by turning red seemingly overnight.

By the time I go to collect a few decorative sprigs in early December, there will already be a resident mistle thrush. His favourite perch is near the crown to gain a good vantage point. He sits here like a miser crouched over his hoard, jealously watching for thieves or rivals which may try to steal his crown. At my approach he flies off giving his characteristic rattling calls of alarm towards the row of neighbouring pines. He perches there and with binoculars I can just make him out staring warily at me, filled with terrors that his jewelled kingdom might be raided in his absence.

He is not always in the holly, however, sometimes he is lurking among the 'sallies' (goat willows) that straggle along the banks of the nearby stream. This probably indicates the proximity of a sparrowhawk or goshawk, and he's waiting for the danger to pass. Normally he's a pugnacious fellow, fiercely defending his scarlet treasure from a host of increasingly hungry thieves. His greatest ire is reserved for sexual rivals, but he will defend his prize from smaller redwings and fieldfares, doves and even wood pigeons. He does this by intimidation rather than actual violence, flying at them only to veer off at the last second. At stake is not just a precious food supply at the leanest time of year, but the implications this has for the breeding season ahead. The fatter and fitter he is at winter's end, the better his chances of attracting the best mate, for any bird that can finish the lean months in good condition is clearly a good breeding prospect. So he spends the winter fighting for food and sex.

By Christmas tawny owls are also beginning to stake out breeding territories, hooting out their instantly recognisable 'too-whit, too-woo' calls and at about the same point the garden robins become increasingly evident. The clichéd seasonal card image of a robin on a snow-covered spade handle as a representation of the season of goodwill and peace couldn't be further from the truth. These are testosterone-pumped pugilists, determined to fight all rivals. At first they are driven by the need to protect their food supplies and territories and will pick fights with any other robin –

even potential future mates. Once, after a heavy snow fall, I was looking at the crowds of finches, tits and nuthatches hanging on the feeders outside the kitchen window when my eye was caught by flying puffs of snow on the back lawn. Two robins were scrapping in the soft powder, bouncing into view as they pecked and kicked in fury, only to sink almost out of sight whenever they paused. No sooner had the last tiny crystals fallen back, however, than the furious tussle would resume.

I couldn't tell what had triggered the violent outburst, but it was probably territorial – maybe a dispute over the pickings beneath the feeders – and the warriors could have been of either sex for both males and females are equally aggressive. Although I've never seen it, there are stories of robins attacking red cloth on the washing line – which would be a far more accurate phrase than the 'red rag to a bull' cliché, for cattle are colour blind.

Blackbirds also get excitable at dusk, even in the depths of winter, with the males declaring their ownership of a territory by angrily chinking at nearby rivals. Noisy squabbles break out in the dense scrub above the hopelessly overgrown rockery we established soon after our arrival. The birds seem to have a particular love of the dogwood that thrives there, no doubt because they grow in dense thickets with plentiful foliage throughout the spring and summer which provides ideal nest sites out of view of thieving magpies. I am always surprised in autumn when the leaves drop to see how many mud and hay cups nestle among the deep red twigs. When I moved here it was with romantic visions of falconry on horseback, riding across the snow-covered hills with my hawk on my fist, faithful hound trotting alongside. I saw myself as some sort of Mongolian eagle-hunter, spending the day out on the hillside to return to a warm fire burning in the hearth and the romance of being snowed in.

That vision was particularly appealing when I was ensconced in a centrally-heated Home Counties house, but the reality is rather different. For a start when you live up a mile of relatively steep winding lane, half of which is privately owned, it only takes an inch or two of snow to be marooned.

Despite having experienced the realities for a quarter of a century, such considerations still don't matter when I hear snow is on its way. There is a sense of excitement – have we enough basic essentials? How do our stores of food, milk and wine look? And the chore of ferrying logs across the yards from the stacks in the barn opposite to fill up the two huge baskets by each fire has an extra sense of satisfaction. I have two huge four-wheeled garden trolleys for this and every afternoon bring across load after load. On a normal winter's day two loads – roughly 50kg – is enough, but in cold weather the stoves gobble up the wood at a phenomenal rate. When temperatures dip below zero four loads barely last a day and a half.

Snow makes these trips all the more onerous, crunching through inches of scrunching white to fill the trolleys, only to find the trudge back through the slippery goo or slush all the harder. Thus I stock up early, the adrenalin rising, like a child on Christmas Eve. What will I wake up to in the morning?

And there it is! A white blanket covers everything, coating lawn, lane and the surrounding hills. My first instinct is to look at the twigs and branches of the hedges and trees. Do they have a covering? Will it last? One of the best indicators is whether it sticks on the roofs and hedges. If so, we have snow for at least a day or so, if not, it is melting fairly fast and soon there will be thin spikes of green showing through the blanket on the lawn.

A striking aspect of new-fallen snow is the silence: a scientist would say this is because the crystals smother noise, stopping the bouncing of invisible sound waves. But there is more to it than that. One of Richard Adams's more astute observations in *Watership Down* is when he observes that when humans say they like bad weather, what they really mean is that they like the sensation of being wrapped up warm and safe. There is certainly something deeply comforting in looking out at a blizzard or driving rain while snuggled up next to a roaring log burner. But the reality of struggling through drifts to feed stock or to reach the main road to stock up with supplies means snow rapidly loses much of its romantic appeal.

One has only to look at the almost mawkish news coverage of tropical storms or the latest ice storm or polar inversion somewhere else in the world. And the almost inevitable heavy snowfall once or twice a year somewhere in Britain provokes an even stronger reaction. News broadcasts are filled with footage of cars sliding across barely white roads or valiant citizens shovelling snow off pavements.

Now nothing we ever experience in Britain compares with the reality of the genuinely Arctic extremes encountered on the two vast landmasses to our east and west. Apart from possibly experiencing relatively mild travel disruption or maybe missing a couple of days work, most people are not seriously inconvenienced by winter weather. After all most of us live in cities, towns or large villages, are on mains gas and electricity and the local shops have sufficient warehouse space to feed the community for at least a week or two.

Yet the more rural you live, the fewer the safety nets. Within a few months of arriving in a relatively remote homestead, I had made sure that we always had a freezer full of food and a cupboard with plenty of dry and tinned produce, but heat can be a very different matter. Oil – the staple heating source for most really rural

Welsh homesteads – has a nasty habit of running out at the beginning of a cold snap and the heavy tankers that bring in fresh supplies will always be the last vehicles to make it back up the lane. Thus almost all have plentiful supplies of firewood in a barn, even if they rarely light the fire. And many others may now rely on an electric cooker and oil-fired central heating, yet the unused Rayburn or Aga remains in the kitchen, cold and unlit, but lurking in reserve, the slumbering dragon waiting to be fired up to rescue the household from the worst.

Our first experience of snowfall came two months after our arrival. It was late February 1994 and there was a six-inch fall of snow that left us totally marooned in a sea of white, criss-crossed with stark black hedges and the dormant winter skeletons of oaks and ash. I was utterly entranced by the sight – it was stunningly beautiful and I instantly took up my hawk and called the dogs out to go hawking.

I soon found, however, that the romance wasn't quite as wonderful as in my dreams. There was nothing at all to hunt for a start. Every rabbit and squirrel was tucked snugly away in a burrow, hole or drey and worse, walking through the six-inch deep powder snow was hard work. All the same I struggled up to the top of the hill to survey the stunning beauty of the views down the Wye Valley and across to Radnor Forest while the dogs bounded around in ecstasy, but after an hour my double-socked feet inside dry wellies were aching with cold and I was tired and very slightly disappointed. There was an uncomfortable discrepancy between my dreams and the reality.

I returned home to find my eight-month pregnant partner very much less impressed by the romance of the situation. Already past the stage where walking was a mild effort even in ideal conditions along a level surface, she had no interest in wandering through the winter wonderland and had more practical issues at the front of her mind. She had spent the morning huddled under a duvet next to the barely-warm stove (the only fuel we could source on our arrival in the middle of a very wet winter had been soaking wet reject softwood planks from a local sawmill). She was also very concerned by the knowledge that we were snowed in – there was no way our little Peugeot 205 could leave the yard, let alone make it down the lane. She intimated in no uncertain terms that the idea of going into premature labour marooned on a mountainside where even the emergency services would struggle to arrive ... well, let's say the concept perturbed her considerably.

That night was frosty in more than one sense and there wasn't the slightest hint of a thaw the next morning – the snow still clung to every branch and twig. Help came from an unexpected direction. As I balefully contemplated the drifts stretching down the lane – it doesn't take more than a breath of wind to puff powder snow into the hollows of a rural track to double the normal depth – I heard the sound of a distant engine.

A tractor was chugging up the lane. It was our neighbour, a huge black plastic bale of haylage impaled on a spike on the front of his tractor and two more stuck on the rear. He was taking a short cut through our yard to get to his sheep in the field below and I waved and nodded as he approached. He stopped and opened the cab door, a rollie cigarette hanging out of his mouth.

'Hello Ernie,' I said.

'How bist ee?'

'I bist fine,' I replied, rather pleased I'd managed to pick up a tiny bit of Radnorshire dialect and also knowing that every time the phrase came out of my rather plummy Oxford mouth it made locals laugh.

He did indeed laugh. 'I just can't understand your accent,' he said. 'But I thought you might like these.' He reached inside the cab and pulled out a jerry can and a litre of milk.

'Two stroke for the saw and milk for you,' he said simply. 'There are a couple of old pallets in the shed down that the bottom of the valley. I'll bring them back for you – they're bone dry and will kick out heat.'

I thanked him and sure enough he was back in a few minutes with not two but four old pallets. He also promised to pull the car out the following morning and get it down to the road if we were still stranded despite the predicted thaw. Fortunately the snows retreated quickly, but the 48-hour scare resulted in some rapid changes. I bought a very old and very thirsty, Series One Land Rover and I found a large second hand freezer in the small ads and located a local woodsman who had some relatively seasoned logs at a reasonable price.

That was just the first occurrence. The following year I was just as excited by the first heavy snow fall – and its successor; and the one after that. It hasn't changed over a quarter of a century. Each time we have a decent fall, I am overjoyed at seeing my world instantly transformed from green to white within hours or even minutes. This is always relatively transitory: the morning is wonderful, charging around the garden taking spectacular photos of the virgin snow while dogs or children bound around, every bit as excited by the wonderful new world.

The dogs are at first taken aback by strange white stuff and dragging their mouths through the upper layers to taste and sense true cold. Puppies are most enjoyable of all to watch. They are first puzzled by this utterly strange new world, particularly when, as they make their first tentative steps, they find the ground giving way beneath them and they sink up to their chests. But gradually they too realise that bounding through the chilly deep carpet is fun. They stick their noses into the powder only to withdraw quickly, sneezing out the flakes and then launching into a pogo-ing series of spirals across the lawn. Better, still, unlike human youngsters, they don't suddenly flip into the early stages of hypothermia, but instead when they get cold they simply run faster to build up body temperature. Meanwhile the children throw themselves into snowball fights, sledging and making snowmen until, inevitably, they are suddenly overcome with the realisation they are cold and have to retreat inside, scattering trails of snow and leaving doors wide open as they rush to warm themselves in front of the fire.

All this joy is infectious and I invariably love the first five or six hours of snow. Indeed, even cooking is more enjoyable – the cold inspires 'warm' dishes such as thick soups, rich red meat casseroles flavoured with porcini accompanied by mounds of mashed potato, polenta or gorgeously thick ribbons of pasta. When children are in the house, the afternoon is spent roasting chestnuts, or communal sessions in the kitchen, with flour slowly dusting everything as we make dumplings, cakes and biscuits.

This mix of gastronomy and freezing conditions leads to evening drinks that I would never consider at any other time of year. Hot toddies made with lemon, our own honey and whisky or rum, or mulled wine: a bottle of cheap red perked up with the addition of cinnamon, nutmeg, cloves and a twist or two of citrus peel. Indeed, I have even been known to take Dickensian inspiration to heat tankards of cider, brandy, lemon and honey with pokers taken red-hot from the fire.

But at some point – and it is generally sooner than one expects – the realities start to sneak in. Cold is pernicious and generally starts with the feet. Once these get cold then the chill seems so sneak up the bones and one's whole body feels frozen and, however cosy the house, the only way to warm up properly is to have a hot bath or scalding shower.

At about this point even I start to contemplate an escape. A short wander along the lane reveals the snow depth and it doesn't take much for the result to be daunting. As often as not it will be beyond most cars. Surprisingly even four-wheel drives such as Land Rovers struggle with relatively small falls, particularly when it has drifted. The presence of children is an additional factor. It is one thing for an adult to flounder the mile down the lane to reach the invariably gritted main road, but quite another to do this with small children. The expedition starts off promisingly enough with laughter and careering races, but the excitement soon wears off. The running jumps into drifts and snowballs means the exuberance quickly turn to complaints about cold feet and demands to be carried.

I now believe the ideal winter should contain two, short, sharp cold snaps with decent falls of heavy snow. Powder may be adored by keen skiers, but they have lifts to whisk them to the top of the mountain and skis to float them back down. Walking through powder is quite another thing. If it's deeper than a couple of inches it quickly becomes hard work, akin to ploughing through boggy ground. And regardless of footwear and clothing, it gets everywhere. It works its way into wellies where it soon melts to soak socks and create the perfect foot freezing conditions.

That said, in a quarter of a century there have been two really hard winters which, in their extremity, were actually enjoyable. The snow came down and on the first I was living on my own with, for once, a four-wheel drive road car which could also cope with snow – an old Subaru. It was perhaps a little thirstier than I might like, but then again it had only cost £400. I soon discovered that it could be trusted to get through all but the deepest snowdrifts and, better still, it never skidded. I had no partner shivering in the background and thus no sense that I was being blamed for the situation. The land was blanketed with white for about three straight weeks on each occasion and I was free to write and to explore the frozen countryside at will.

Another benefit of long-lasting snow is the chance to track local wildlife. Rabbits, hares and woodcock might spend the first couple of days hidden away in cosy lairs, but after a day or two are driven by hunger to leave their burrows and sheltered nooks. And this can produce surprises. For example, during most winters our local rabbits disappear almost completely, yet after four of five days of snow it becomes clear two or three feed regularly on the lawn at night. I have no idea where they are during the day, for there are no evident buries and the dogs keep working their way through the hedges and brash, yet never flush them.

The presence of local foxes making regular trips through the yard was less surprising, but the snow clearly revealed they were being drawn like magnets to the chicken coop, circling the little structure as they probed for weak points. The cold also makes them more audacious and one morning as I wrote an article I looked up to see a large dog trotting around the lawn. Now unlike my neighbours, I don't mind foxes too much, in fact I actually like to see them on the open hill, but I want them to respect certain boundaries.

That said, I have a responsibility to protect my flocks even though I don't have any particular fondness for 'the gals', all of which are now 'spent' layers from local egg farms: birds bought for £1 a time to save them from the abattoir. My attitude stems from years of discovering piles of feathers around the farm after a raider has snatched one of the layers. Over the years this has meant I no longer seek out the beautiful rare breeds that lay beautifully-coloured eggs. Their cheap successors lay happily until, inevitably, they too are seized by a fox in an unguarded moment.

While growing up I had loved seeing the urban foxes in our

North Oxford garden. I respected their intelligence and adaptability to work out how to live alongside man. In the main they add to the quality of life of the citizens. If they spill the contents of a rubbish bag across a footpath or alley, it is really a comment on man's waste and a careless attitude towards the inevitable detritus of modern life.

In contrast a rural fox has thousands of acres across which to roam and very good cause to avoid human habitations. Any brave enough to systematically risk the farmer and his gun has got too brazen for anyone's good I reasoned. It would only be a matter of time before it would find some weak point in the defences and then, in an instant, I would lose what was left of my depleted flock. So I moved the hen house with its occupants – now down to a trio from the original half dozen – to a spot opposite the front door. I decided that, not least thanks to the snow, there was to be no free ranging until the threat from the fox had receded.

But the danger didn't retreat: it became more pressing. For the next two days there were tracks all around the hen house as at least one prowler sniffed for a weak point. Then I got up soon after dawn to look out to see a large dog fox patrolling around the run while the three hens squawked frantically in a mixture of outrage and terror.

I ran to the gun cabinet and pulled out my rifle – small-calibre .22 which I had bought solely to control rabbits on the lawn and squirrels on the bird feeders. It is rarely used, for I don't particularly enjoy shooting, but now was an appropriate moment. Slipping the magazine full of tiny brass bullets into the gun, I opened the front door ever so slowly and raised it to my shoulder. I am not a crack shot, but it wasn't a difficult target and a split second later I heard the unmistakeable sound of the bullet hitting its chest. The fox leaped a couple of feet in the air and was then off, running frantically across the yard towards the open fields. My heart sank – had I only wounded it? This was terrible! But a moment later I relaxed as the creature suddenly slowed and then tumbled over onto its side. I pulled on my wellies and, still in my dressing gown, ran across to it.

The fox was stunningly beautiful as it lay, deep, rusty red, against the snow, its mouth slightly open in that characteristic vulpine grin. And it was the deep, dark, dry red of the pelt which was most striking – as beautiful a shade as anyone might imagine and far more appealing than the thin trickle of bright scarlet blood trickling from beneath his tongue.

I stood there; conflicted. I felt no triumph at having taken this life, but I was relieved I had killed humanely, rather than let him run away to die from gangrene. At the same time I was filled with a sense of sorrow. If only he and his kind could not give my homestead a hundred-yard berth we could have lived and let lived.

I knew his mate would probably already be pregnant, ready to rear her young at the top of the field or in my new-planted wood. The post script to this story, however, was that a couple of months later, when the grass had just started to grow and the buds were breaking in the hedgerows, I released the remaining chickens from their pen to wander at will around the garden and, sure enough, within a few weeks they had all gone, snatched no doubt, by a nearby nursing vixen – quite probably his mate – desperate to feed her cubs. I have always thought February was the most depressing month of the year. The predominant weather seems to be chilly, grey and damp. Everything looks untidy – tussocky washed out grass, mud everywhere, while trees and hedges stand like parading skeletons across the landscape.

And yet new life is stirring and starting to thrust its way into the light. The clichéd starters are the snowdrops which can begin to emerge soon after the New Year, but they are quickly followed by crocuses – pretty to view, but in the end both are a little disappointing to the naturalist because they stem from human plantings. Rather more exciting are the profusion of catkins bursting forth on hazels and 'sallies'. These little lamb tails of flowers are very variable. Someone once told me cobs only flower in profusion every two to three years. If true, this puts them in the same category as oaks which produce bumper crops of acorns sporadically, as if saving up their reserves for one explosion which is so prolific that the jays and squirrels cannot possibly harvest them all.

Another early sign of the imminent reproductive explosion is the sudden appearance of toads and frogs. The first sight is usually on the lane after dark when headlights show the tarred surface dotted with hopping frogs and lumbering toads. A couple of days later the pond becomes a veritable Jacuzzi as frogs, toads and newts roll and grapple in a procreative orgy amid the watercress and weed.

This puzzled me for several years. I kept encountering little piles of translucent jelly on top of fence posts and stumps. I racked my brain looking for a plausible source. There were various possibilities, including slime moulds, but somehow they didn't look quite right. To start with, they cropped up on such a wide range of 'hosts' – rocks, treated timber and even in grass. The goo looked like wallpaper paste, randomly piped out of an icing bag by some invisible deranged witch or druid. Indeed, when I asked around I discovered it is sometimes called witches paste or star jelly.

I was completely non-plussed by this mysterious apparently synthetic material sitting on rotting fence posts. There seemed no rational explanation. Eventually I stumbled on the answer – it is unfertilised frogspawn and comes from an unfortunate female toad or frog hopping towards a breeding pond. Usually they travel under cover of darkness, but sometimes are so driven by the reproductive urge that they risk travelling across open ground in daylight. This exposes them to the buzzards and crows perched in the hedges. In some cases the prey is devoured *in situ*, in others it was taken it to a convenient minor vantage point where it was safer to deal with the prey while keeping open a beady eye for danger. In either case, the crow or buzzard would discard the jelly to devour the flesh, bones and skin of the unfortunate amphibian. This fastidiousness at first appears odd because, after all, carrion-eaters such as foxes, buzzards and crows are hardly known for being picky eaters, but in fact it isn't really unsurprising. After all one of the jelly's prime roles is to protect the precious embryo within, partially by providing an insulating barrier from the elements, but clearly also by being particularly unpalatable.

All creatures live on the edge, perpetually struggling to find food and to avoid becoming a meal for something else. Due to their nocturnal habits, barn owls are relatively safe from predation, although they are certainly not immune to attacks from tawny owls or a lurking evening goshawk. They are much more sensitive to weather. In long hot summers when the vole population is at one of its cyclical highs, big clutches and a high fledging rate are the norm, meaning the population can more than double in a season. On the other hand, bad weather can very quickly take a terrible toll. Barn owls are not really built for British conditions (the Scottish population is one of the world's most northerly outposts). Their soft plumage acts like a sponge in rain, soaking up moisture. This seriously hampers hunting flights and dramatically increases heat loss.

Cold winters also seriously reduce the available food, as the voles on which they depend hunker down in the warmth of burrows. They will have stashed nuts, berries and seeds in the good times and these come into their own when snow blankets the ground. This drives them even deeper underground and when they do venture to the surface they are protected by a muffling layer as they scuttle along snow tunnels between their stores.

All owls are surprisingly light and spindly beneath the insulating feathered cloak, but barn owls are particularly small. They might appear to be about the same size as a wood pigeon but they weigh less than half as much because they have very little body fat. This and the difficulty of hunting in bad weather means harsh winters can wreak havoc with populations. The infamous winter of 1962-63 devastated Britain's barn owl population, although 1947 was worse in Wales. More recently there were three particularly harsh winters in 2009, 2010 and 2012 and for the next three or four years there was no evidence of their presence in our barns.

The struggles with bad weather can temporarily make the owls much more evident, however. Food is harder to find as the winter ends and the female needs the extra nutrients for what is to come. Egg production is a serious drain because the shells are largely composed of calcium. For owls most of this comes from the bones of their prey, but the huge spike in demand in early spring means they still need to deplete their own skeletons prior to laying. This makes them more fragile than normal and is a major reason why females tend to incubate rather than hunt while the male supplies food – she is protecting herself from harm as she rebuilds her bones.

DOMESTIC WILDLIFE

A large part of the appeal of Tan y Cefn for us was the crumbling former milking parlour stretching west from the main house. It was a long sprawling building some sixty yards long and twenty feet wide. It was first a dairy, then housed beef cattle before serving as trekking stables and then housed battery chickens. By the time we bought the house it was in a dreadful condition. We'd always vaguely that we might convert it but funds were short and we had no need of the extra room. This changed one stormy night in 1998 when there was a loud bang. The next morning we discovered an entire corner had collapsed, toppling five tonnes of masonry into the yard. The idea of this happening while the two children were playing below was enough to spur action and within weeks we were trying to find a builder prepared to take on the work.

This proved near impossible because those we approached took the briefest of glances at the building before pronouncing it beyond repair. Their inevitable advice was to demolish the existing barn and to replace it with a timber frame and breeze block structure.

'But it's a beautiful old building,' I protested.

'Well we could stone-clad it,' came the response.

'But look at those fantastic old timbers!' I countered, pointing to the gnarled and twisted oak purlins and trusses, held together with hand-whittled pegs. Looking up was to stare into history – the irregularities of the beams clearly showed they had been hand rather than machine sawn. Indeed most had not been sawn at all, but hacked into shape with an adze. The original workmen had used whatever was available, working *with* the limbs and trunks of trees rather than fighting them. Disciplined regularity only really came into domestic architecture with the invention of steam-powered saws and mass-produced bricks in the eighteenth century. Until then, provided the wood was roughly straight, that was good enough. These curved rafters are often called 'ship timbers' in the belief they are recycled beams taken from boats, but in fact most simply reflect the fact that Britain grows very little decent hardwood.

It takes years of careful management to produce good timber. Trees need to be planted closely and thinned regularly to persuade them to race for the sky, producing straight-grained trunks without side limbs to mar the timber with knots. This is rarely done in Britain where we lost any serious forestry skills we might have had some thousand years ago. In Wales problems are further compounded by the thin, acidic, soil which produces the stunted trees which make the precious hanging oak forests beloved by wildlife and conservationists, but utterly valueless in terms of timber – or at least timber for modern building techniques.

It was not always thus: the roof timbers in the barn clearly showed the ingenuity with which the builders of old used what came to hand. Most of the irregular timbers were oak, but there was some ash and one large timber – probably a nineteenth century repair – was sycamore. The lack of straight lines gave it real character: life even. As I showed the latest builder the exposed beams, I felt like Jonah staring at the ribs of the whale.

'They are nice, yes, but it's far too difficult to save them,' came the reply. 'They are all over the place and it would the devil of a job to pack them out sufficiently to put on new slates.'

'Could the existing slates not be saved?'

'No, they are all sorts of shapes and sizes and because of their age most would probably break. It will be much easier and quicker to use new materials. It will save you a lot of money, believe me,' he said.

This was not at all what I wanted to hear, but the dangerous state of the structure made action imperative. With no builders willing to renovate the structure, we reluctantly began to draw up plans for a conventional breeze block replacement. At the last moment, however, a *deus ex macchina* appeared at the primary school gate. Our son Jack was in year two and his precocious three-year-old sister, Molly, was joining reception classes for a couple of days every week. Both of their classes were suddenly swollen by the arrival of fresh blood in the form of the children of some newcomers to the parish. Gussie joined Jack and Teddy slotted into Molly's group. Naturally we got talking to the new parents and invited them up for a cup of tea.

No sooner than Nick caught sight of the barn he began to inspect the oak framing, running his hands reverentially over the joints and nodding approvingly as he saw the irregular protruding pegs. But when I explained our plans for a replacement his mood changed completely.

'You do that and my children will never speak to yours again,' he said darkly. 'Of course this place can be saved – and I know what I'm talking about, I've taken on much more daunting projects.'

When we paid a return visit to see their home, it was clear he wasn't exaggerating. The couple had moved with their children into a caravan next to a tumbled-down chimney which was all that was left of a farmhouse on the other side of our valley. It was Nick's plan to rebuild this virtually from scratch using traditional green oak framing techniques. The problem was that they were running short of funds for the necessary timber. It didn't take long to start to hatch a plan. Nick said he would produce drawings and make a frame for us, if I paid him a flat fee and provided all the materials. And because we would both save money, he suggested I also buy the oak he needed in lieu of part of the fee. The pair of us sat down and tried to draw up a budget for the scheme and calculated that it couldn't possibly cost more than £30,000, so we added in a healthy margin and decided we'd allow £40,000 to be on the safe side.

This plan also allowed us far more flexibility with our use of the space. Having so recently looked at scores of Welsh farms, I was acutely aware that most old buildings have small rooms. This is, after all, a sensible step when trying to keep warm in pre-central heating properties, but my inclination was very much towards the large. So we decided to leave the eighty-eight foot barn as one huge open-plan room, with a kitchen taking up a third at one end beneath a bedroom and bathroom.

We looked around and were delighted to find a relatively local – and extremely rare – source of British green oak. It came from Shobden, a village only just over the border into Herefordshire and barely half an hour east along the A44. These were still in trunk form when Nick located them which was ideal for it allowed him to place a bespoke order for dozens of beams of assorted lengths and sizes. These arrived a few weeks later and we stacked them in the yard, draping them with a huge blue tarpaulin.

At the same point Nick moved his tools in. He wanted to cut every joint of the oak frame by hand, using drill, hammer and chisel. After a couple of days, however, he said he needed more help than the occasional hour or two that I could spare, so we recruited a young builder, Will, fresh from college. He was intrigued by the idea of learning about 'the vernacular' as Nick insisted on calling the project.

Work progressed as Will and Nick selected beams to fit each

gap or rotten timber. The uprights were six inches square and ten feet high. Purlins were four inches square and sixteen feet long, the two huge beams to support the bedroom and bathroom were eight inches by six inches and carefully spliced together. Every joint was carefully tailored, each cut to suit its location. Thus some ends had to be cut square, in other places the mortices and tenons were sawn at tailored angles to fit the existing frame. Every tenon and matching cavity were tailor-made. Precision cutting was important because each junction had to have the tightest of fits.

There then followed the laborious process of ensuring the two could be connected as they lay on the floor. First they would be lined up and any excess would be shaved from the tenon by pushing a wide chisel up its sides until it just about fitted. Its sides would then be waxed with a candle stub before the two huge beams were forced together using an ingenious set up of webbing straps twisted tight with a crowbar or winched into place with a car jack providing the power. Once a satisfactorily tight joint had been achieved, the two would be pulled apart before the two beams, each weighing as much as four or five men, were hauled into their final positions where the joint would be reassembled – inevitably accompanied by much cursing and bruised fingers.

The next stage was to drill a hole through the joint. Or rather to make two holes, one from either side, each at the gentlest of downward sloping angles. These would meet in the middle of the tenon. At this point a long whittled oak peg, slightly larger in diameter than the hole, would also be waxed and hammered into the hole. The whittling – as opposed to lathing – means the peg has ridges which grip the walls of the hole and the slightly elliptical nature of the tunnel means it's bent as it is hammered in. As a result, once it has been banged home it is held irrevocably in place – there is no hope of hammering it back out. Any mistakes have to be drilled out and a new, larger peg will have to be whittled for the repair.

The same building technique gave us one of the first significant indications of the true age of at least some parts of the house. We knew it could not pre-date the seventeenth century, because before that Welsh buildings were 'cruck framed' – built with curved beams leaning in on each other – but these timbers were also in high demand by the burgeoning Tudor navy, so shorter, straighter sawn timbers took over, with more structural strength placed on stone walls and also marked by steeper roofs.

The age of the main house is impossible to divine with accuracy – it was clearly old because the walls were built of stone rather than brick and the lines were clearly too irregular to have been built after the late-eighteenth century. One or two huge beams and the thickness of the walls suggested large parts must pre-date this, but then again, there was a brick bread oven which was clearly Victorian. In other words, as with most local farmhouses, an old house had been periodically added to by successive owners over the centuries.

Some of these additions were uncovered as Nick and Will worked away at the restoration. As they inspected old joints for signs of weakness, they came across ancient carpenter's marks on the roof trusses. These took the form of a strange series of slashes and circles; each mirrored either side of a joint. They denote which timber fits with which, for while Nick and Will were constructing the frame on site, the original would probably have been constructed elsewhere and brought up as a kit by cart. Then as today it would be heaved into place and reassembled, the joints hammered together with waxed oak pegs.

The significance of the marks, according to this lover of vernacular buildings, is that in the early eighteenth century, growing literacy meant Welsh builders switched from these primitive symbols to Roman numerals. In other words, the marks point strongly to the barn being seventeenth century in origin and possibly making it older than the adjoining building.

The optimistic projections which marked my early discussion with Nick went the way of all building projects. The work progressed slowly and like all 'grand designs' things went wrong and the time flew by while costs escalated. Instead of five months and £30,000, after a year and a half I found I'd run up bills of £80,000 – but at least I had a palace and, according to the Institute of Surveyors, had still done the restoration for a third of official price.

One of the side effects of these traditional techniques is that they lend themselves to wildlife-friendly twists. During the conversion Nick made a measuring error with one beam and only discovered his mistake after cutting four mortices. Naturally we adopted a 'vernacular' approach and found an alternative use for the sixteen foot timber. It ended up as an exposed wallplate under the overhanging roof with the holes facing down. My first instinct was to plug these, but Will had a better idea and three-quarter filled the gap, leaving a small aperture with a six by three inch hole within. These are now used by local wrens as winter roosts and I have sat quietly with a cup of tea on a sofa by the window at dusk, counting up to half a dozen small bodies flitting into just one hole.

Swallows also find the restored building too tempting to resist. Throughout spring and summer any open window or door is an open invitation for an adult looking for a new nest site or just curious fledglings wanting to explore. Once in they become disoriented and fly around, twittering frantically, as they look for an exit and ushering the uninvited and twittering incomers out is a daily chore. They aren't difficult to catch in the rooms in the old house, but things are more tricky in the barn conversion where they fly back and forth among the beams, some fifteen feet above the flagstones. The answer then is to open the two skylights in the upstairs bedroom and bathroom and then to try to herd them towards that end of the barn by waving arms and calling loudly.

They are not the only aerial visitors. A year after finishing the conversion I noticed tiny black flecks on the floor. They looked like mouse droppings, but were clustered rather than randomly scattered. Mice leave tiny black packages wherever they go, but this is generally under furniture, or along the relative safety of walls. In contrast these droppings were grouped in the middle of the room and surrounded by the debris of orange moth wings. That left bats as the obvious source.

Apparently you can also tell the difference by rolling the droppings between your fingers. Mouse droppings have a higher moisture content so break down into an oily smear. In contrast those from a bat are crumbly – dusty even. I didn't particularly fancy the experiment, so instead looked up, but could see nothing. Clearly they had squeezed into a crack above the beam and were nestled out of sight. Over the subsequent weeks I would sweep up the little black offerings every few days and find them rapidly replenished, so clearly the bats were very present and there were several of them too. After another week or two I found another little collection of droppings at the other end of the barn. I searched around the place trying to work out how they were getting in and out and eventually found a suitable opening above the porch that would easily allow access to a bat.

But despite knowing of their presence, for at least a couple of years I never saw one in the barn although there were usually several fluttering around outside from an hour before dusk and early in the morning. There were at least two species for there was an evident size disparity, but beyond this I was at a loss as visual identification is no easy matter. Obviously they fly in poor lighting conditions and Britain has some fifteen species (by far our biggest mammal group). Most of these are present in Wales, so there were at least half-a-dozen likely contenders. I invited the local bat recorder to visit with a detector, but she dragged her heels and I grew bored of badgering her.

I also knew I had further colonies outside under the weather-boarding. There was one small roost above the backdoor, again evident from the droppings below. In that case they were getting in and out from the very bottom through a two inch gap between wall and boards. With the help of a torch I could peer up to see half a dozen little creatures clustered together in the dark. On another occasion I was up just before dawn in late summer and went outside to see dozens of bats swooping around the weather end of the house, flying up to the boards only to wheel away at the last moment. Their behaviour was most reminiscent of excited swallows or martins starting to flock prior to migration. As I watched, their numbers began to drop off. Clearly they were landing and scuttling in under the boards although they achieved this so quickly that, hard as I stared, I didn't see it actually happen until the very end when, with only a couple of the fluttering creatures to watch, it was easier to concentrate on one animal. Inside the droppings ceased to appear in November. The residents had clearly departed for the winter, but they were back next year, however, and back again the year after.

Eventually I worked out their identity, although unfortunately not in the way I would have liked. My teenage daughter pestered and pestered me to be allowed a cat. I've never been a feline fan because I see them as inveterate wildlife killers, but eventually I succumbed to the pressure and we got a lithe kitten found dumped by a bottle bank. At first she was nothing but a delight, but in time her instincts came the fore and she started to bring in a growing tally of small creatures. First there were the insects and spiders, then various amphibians, shrews and voles and I was becoming increasingly unhappy with the death toll.

Things deteriorated even further when she killed two swallows. But the last straw came when she learned about the barn's bats. Clearly she had discovered the hole above the door and would sit there, swiping them with her needle-tipped paws as they entered or left the building. She left the corpses in the kitchen, four in five days. I was really upset – but at least I could check their identity. They were brown long-eared bats.

The diminutive size of the bats under the weather boards meant they were almost certainly pipistrelles and a few months later I noticed tell-tale streaks on some of the internal walls in the barn opposite. Eventually I bullied the local bat recorder to visit and she confirmed the presence of brown long-eared bats in the barn, pipistrelles under the weather boarding and said the streaks in the outbuildings were noctules.

There are other surprise visitors, more often than not during what I like to call a Welsh summer. October weather is often some of the best, with warm sunny days and glorious misty mornings. In such conditions I often sleep with the bedroom window open, enjoying the fresh air, birdsong and the musty scents of 'mellow fruitfulness'. This can produce surprises, however. Occasionally a bat will fly in only to circle in panic when it cannot find the way out. As a child I could hear their ultrasonic squeaks around our Oxfordshire cottage, but have long-since lost that ability. The bigger bats – particularly the brown long-eareds – are still comparatively noisy in a confined space, their rapid wing beats making a loud whirring as they whirl around the lightshade. Once woken by this

– and I am a light sleeper – the only solution is to persuade the intruder to leave. The butterfly net which might catch a moth or bird is useless with a bat because its sonar allows it to dodge this with ease. Thus it is a case of either waiting until it finds the open window or for it to land. When clinging to a wall, curtain or beam it is much is easier to catch in a swoop of bare hands. This risks a nip, but it is then the work of a couple of seconds to throw it out of the window.

Sometimes the intruder is bigger. One night I was woken in the small hours by a light blow on the chest. I woke with a start, thinking that either a child or the dog was on the bed, but when I turned on the bedside lamp, I found myself staring at the owl. I had fed her two chicks on my outstretched palm the previous night, but no doubt the dropping temperature and nip in the air had left her disappointed.

WILDLIFE ON THE MOVE

Really cold weather might be unpleasant for humans, but we can always shelter in homes that are at least dry and we have ways of heating even the oldest and draughtiest buildings. Yes, in extremis we might have to shut internal doors, retreating to the warmest room during the as daylight fades. Then at night the fallbacks are hot water bottles, high tog duvets, with extra blankets and throws, but at least we avoid life-threatening cold and have plenty of food in the store cupboards and freezers.

Life is not so simple for most wildlife. True, many insects, amphibians, reptiles and some mammals can resort to dormancy or even hibernation. For creatures such as slugs and toads this is a relatively risk-free strategy. They need do little more than find a secure cranny where they are unlikely to be found and then just sink into deep torpor. If there is a warm spell, they may emerge to quest for food or mating opportunities, but should the weather turn cold again, they simply repeat the exercise.

True hibernation is far more risky for mammals such as bats, dormice and hedgehogs. These face greater challenges. Firstly, as warm blooded creatures, they need to have laid down several months' worth of fat reserves before they start the deep sleep. Once fully asleep, their breathing and heart beats slow to barely ticking over and their body temperature drops to a few degrees above freezing. While they sleep they are totally defenceless, yet they still represent valuable calorie-rich food packages for predators such as foxes or pine martens.

Thus hedgehogs and dormice rely on leaf and grass-stuffed hidey-holes tucked into hedgebottoms or tree hollows. Bats adopt a very different strategy. Rather than seek cosiness, they look for caves, abandoned tunnels or hollow trees. Unlike other hibernating mammals, they are not after the insulation of a snug leaf-lined bed: indeed their chosen retreats are usually distinctly cool. To look for conditions resembling those of a kitchen fridge might seem counter intuitive, but in fact they are just trying to avoid one of the most energy-intensive risks for any hibernating animal: to wake prematurely. The process of dropping into – or lifting out of – suspended animation burns up a lot of energy. A bat which wakes up in mid-winter to fly around hunting non-existent insects will, in one day, burn off the calories that would sustain it for a fortnight's hibernation. Despite this, bats will wake up to hunt in warm weather in mid-winter. Indeed, when I eventually spotted the resident bats flitting around the living room it was on New Year's Eve.

Being far more mobile, birds have other options – they can simply flee from harsh conditions. In some cases these journeys are relatively short-distance, so curlew and golden plover leave the uplands for the milder conditions of the frost-free coastal mud flats and salt marshes. Naturally, the presence of huge flocks of waders and waterfowl along the coast also attracts predators, so the peregrines, merlins, harriers and short-eared owls that have preyed on them all summer soon follow.

Half our breeding birds take a completely different approach to cold weather. They simply bail out and migrate to a warmer climate. Autumn is a time both of plenty and of flux. While the oaks are laden with acorns above fungi-strewn woodland floors as hedgerows heave with fruit and berries, so half most birds are straining to leave for pastures new.

By September the skies are resounding with the sound of excited chattering of swallows, manically darting over the lawn and clearly more interested in conveying their adrenaline-pumped mood to their peers than in catching late summer insects.

As the days go by, the frantic mood begins to slow as the birds interrupt their flights to perch on roofs and wires. The numbers build up slowly, starting with small groups of parents and their last brood, but they are soon joined by others. It might be sentimental to suggest these are earlier clutches from the past few months, but it's not too whimsical. Whatever the case, quite soon the lines of noisy birds perched on phone wires are far too great for these to be the offspring of one pair. There can easily be a hundred perched on the wires outside Pen y Banc ('top of the bank'), a farm halfway down the lane towards Rhayader, chirping frenetically to their neighbours, as the ever-swelling tribes start to work themselves up for their flight to South Africa. It is as if they know the eight thousand mile journey is going to be so arduous and perilous that they need each other's support to psyche themselves up to fever pitch. Day by day the long-tailed chattering dots string out further and further and grow ever more noisy ... and then one day there is silence. The glistening blue, red-throated, streamer-tailed birds that have delighted me all summer have suddenly vanished.

The swallows and martins are just the most conspicuous members of the exodus. Whilst we humans are staring up at the excited crowds on the phone lines, we fail to notice the sudden dearth of movement in the hedgerows. The warblers, flycatchers and redstarts have already quietly departed, flying off towards the south coast singly or in small groups. They will briefly refresh with a last feed before launching off again across the Bay of Biscay for southern France or Spain before continuing to Morocco on their way to their final destination in Gambia or Senegal.

For many centuries amateur naturalists were bemused by their sudden disappearance at the end of summer. Where could they all have gone? Many of Europe's top naturalists believed Aristotle's speculating that swallows might hibernate in the mud at the bottom of ponds. Indeed Gilbert White is often undermined as a great naturalist because he is supposed to have been an adherent of this still widely-accepted theory. This is unfair. White merely refers to it as an idea and while he doesn't scoff, he doesn't endorse it.

We now know the mass autumnal departure of half of Wales's summer bird population is simply down to calories. The protein-rich insects on which most depend are sparse in a Welsh winter, but abundant in the warmth of southern Europe or, more usually, sub-Saharan Africa. The alternative seeds and fruits to which many can turn outside the breeding season are also in increasingly short supply. To compound the problems, shorter days mean there is much less time to find food, while cold wet weather doubles the need for energy.

Yet migration is far from risk free and the flight south is a calculated gamble. Taking on the journey is a major feat for such small creatures: swallows, for example, weigh about the same as two pound coins, yet have to fly eight thousand miles to over-winter in South Africa. All the way they are risking storms, predators, drought and starvation. Yet those that remain also have to be tough, for as well as far less food, the smaller birds are deprived of cover and thus far more at the mercy of predators.

The sudden quiet once they have departed does not last long. Within a couple of weeks the bubbling torrent of excited swallow calls is replaced by the harsher noises of winter visitors, for while winter in the mountains of Wales may be too harsh for many songbirds, conditions seem positively tropical to birds who've spent the summer rearing young in Scandinavia.

The first to arrive are generally redwings, small cousins of the song thrush. As so often with winter migrants, the absence of the territorial breeding imperative means these are far more gregarious by nature than their resident cousins. Redwings get their name from the flash of red feathers under their wings – although these are disappointingly difficult to see unless you get a good view as they feed on the branches or feast on a rotting windfall full of worms and beetles. They are relatively shy, but every October they fill the overgrown hedges festooned with scarlet and orange hawthorn and rowan berries. Then, as I drive home, flocks will suddenly erupt from the foliage. They leave not in the sudden simultaneous panicked burst of thousands of waders on the shore, but sequentially in twos and threes until some thirty or forty have departed to fly on ahead, only for the pattern to be repeated a hundred yards further down the road.

A week or two later, they will be joined by the biggest of the thrushes, fieldfares, fleeing the first frosts and snows of a Swedish winter. Capped and tailed with the dashing blue-grey of a Prussian soldier, they also like to flock along the lanes to dine on the suddenly obvious rosehips and spindle. This ripening fruit has been there for weeks, but the berries were obscured by foliage. Then the first storms of winter arrive to strip the last leaves from the branches, often doing their work overnight to leave glistening black twiggy fingers adorned with a handful of garish berries and making the thrushes all the more conspicuous.

One a decade the hedges will also be brightened by the orange-pink plumage of flocks of waxwings, driven west by harsh Continental weather. Every year hundreds of these handsome crested birds cross the North Sea from Central Europe, but they generally stay along the east coast. Every few years a particularly harsh burst of weather drives flocks many thousands strong across the waves. This 'irruption' can then ripple across the country, stripping hedgerows and coppices of their over-ripe fruit. About five years ago there was one and, advised by Caroline, I rushed to a local pub to see a couple of dozen of these garish finches dining on the bright red rowan berries in the car park. Two days later the trees were bare and the birds had disappeared to the south west.

The visitors augment plenty of resident species which are prepared to stick the winter out. These have to make the best of the available natural shelter. The dense bamboo clump next to the pond, for example, is evergreen and in winter at dusk it positively shakes with little bodies settling down for the night. Bigger birds such as pigeons, corvids and buzzards generally roost along the edges of conifer plantations, but the local kites prefer communal roosts in the bare branches of an isolated oak or ash. And the normally territorial and aggressive wren will take things even further, snuggling up with others to share warmth in a nest box, cavity or, as already mentioned, in the cavities Will created in the wallplate.

Barn owls obviously live up to their name by readily turning to man for shelter. They have a marked inclination to take shelter in buildings and even a semi-derelict ruin will have snug corners offering shelter from the worst of the wind, rain and snow. Although they prefer the privacy of a building which is abandoned or rarely used, they are surprisingly good at melting into the shadows even in a store which is visited daily. My male vanishes outside the breeding season, although I occasionally disturb him in one of the woodsheds, but the female is much less concerned by human activity. She moves from the now ammonia-laden atmosphere of the nest box to roost in the garage on the other side of the lane. Her preferred perch is on a beam next to a cavity between the corrugated iron roof and the ceiling and she will sit there staring at me as I rummage for tools, although when I start up a drill or saw, the noise is too much and she vanishes into the hole.

HISTORY AND NATURE

The local landscape is pock-marked with the remains of man's environmental exploitation. The general conviction of most people that our green fields and purple-clad moors are natural and untouched always amuses me. However rural an area might appear, every British landscape actually bears the marks of seven millennia of man's presence. Be they moorland, forest, fields, hedges or drystone walls, our most precious habitats are manmade, but most people are reluctant to recognise this. Instead we have a desperate urge to romanticise the landscape.

Our area is sometimes described as one of the few places in Britain which has completely missed the polluting influence of the Industrial Revolution. The landscape has been moulded by centuries of farming and apparently little else. Its towns would be described as villages or even hamlets anywhere else in Britain and even today there are virtually no factories or big employers. It seems pure: unpolluted, natural and organic.

The reality is very different. This area actually experienced its Industrial Revolution before almost anywhere else in Britain. In fact the process was grinding to a halt here just as things were taking off along the Pennines and Midlands. The earliest mines in Mid-Wales are thousands of years old. Some are Neolithic and the Romans mined the Cambrians for silver and gold, but the heyday came in the seventeenth and eighteenth centuries. For a century or two the area was the world's richest source of copper and tin. As a result Britain's richest man at the turn of the eighteenth and nineteenth centuries was Thomas Johns, a member of the Here-fordshire gentry who inherited a selection of mines scattered around Devil's Bridge. He was only the country's wealthiest man for a brief period because he spent his entire fortune on his estate at Hafod, constructing a huge house with the biggest private library in the world.

Mining continued to be an important source of income for landowners and locals into the early years of the twentieth century. But suddenly a range of factors saw the total collapse of the industry within a matter of a few years. The main cause was a crash in the price of metal as new deposits of more easily-extracted minerals were found around the Empire.

That said, the last workings in the Elan Valley were shut not because they were uneconomic, but to prevent heavy metals contaminating Birmingham's new water supply.

Even today its water needs to be filtered to remove the peat particles which are contaminated with the residues from the mine workings. These are gathered by sitting for three days in huge pools below the last dam prior to their three-day journey to Birmingham. Every few months the tanks are scraped out and a few years ago someone had the idea of selling this in his garden centre, only for the scheme to be scuppered when tests showed the peat is still unsafe to use. A little further to the north west the water runs out of the old workings at Cwmystwyth staining the rocks orange with iron oxide.

As mentioned, the earliest mine workings in Mid-Wales date back 4,100 years, but since then men laboured to wrench copper, lead, tin and silver – plus just a little gold – from the bowels of the earth. They would delve into the soil, hoping to strike a rich pocket of minerals. These were not the deep shafts of the coal mines of South Wales with cages and lifts, but short shafts and tunnels driven perhaps a hundred feet into the rocky soil. The geology meant minerals were deposited in small concentrated pockets. Sometimes the miners would get lucky and hit a particularly rich lode full of a silver and tin mix with up a fifth made up of the precious metal.

This would be broken up with powder, picks and sledgehammers and carried to the surface to be crushed by water-powered rollers and hammers. The resulting powder was then washed and the heavier ore would be separated in settling tanks. Then the concentrate was taken by cart down the valleys to be further refined where there was an easier power source and then on to distant markets, usually by river or sea. Aberystwyth was once one of the busiest ports in Wales thanks to the rich deposits in the Rheidol and Ystwyth valleys. And its links with its industrial past are revealed in local place names. There is a spectacular kite feeding station at Nant yr Arian, for example – which means 'silver stream' because of the precious deposits found there for countless centuries. Another mine a little to the south near Cwmystwyth was known as Silver Mountain until the sixteenth century when new finds saw the name changed to Copper Mountain.

One notable aspect of this industrial past is that unlike the coal mines of South Wales, there was no attempt to return the landscape to its pristine original condition. When the mines were abandoned the miners simply packed up their shovels and picks and walked away. The most dangerous shafts are fenced off to stop sheep from falling in and as a warning to curious walkers, but most are open for anyone to investigate. Not that this would be wise for the timbers supporting the walls and roof in even the most recent are over a century old.

This means that the Cambrians are dotted with signs of the industrial past for those that can read the landscape. Even when shafts have collapsed or been filled in, there are piles of rocks which stand out amid the pale greens and browns of the upland grass. Nearby there will often be the remains of leats dug into the hillsides to channel water between the walls which housed the bucketed wheels. These turned the giant rollers which smashed and crushed the ore. Sometimes there are the ruins of buildings, shelters for the miners or their ponies.

These remnants of the past are a source of fascination for historians. One day in late June, as I filled the car with fuel, the mechanic shyly asked if I was interested in exploring a mine he had just spotted on the internet. He had been pouring over Google Earth's aerial view of the Claerwen Valley and had seen the tell-tale grey splashes of spoil heaps in a little side valley. I was flattered and readily agreed. The next day I met David and his regular mine investigating partner, Vic. We drove as far up a rough track as we could and then walked the last couple of miles.

The place was utterly deserted apart from the inevitable sheep, but it was clear we were following more than a sheep track – it was wider and the gradient was comparatively smooth. This had obviously once been a road wide enough to take a cart. It might even have been railed. Beneath us and on the hill sides opposite there were scatterings of stone, splashes of grey across the grass. Some were relatively small – the spoil from trial shafts dug into the hills and rapidly abandoned, others were far bigger and denoted proper workings. Towards the top of the valley there were signs of water wheels, the only source of power in these coal-less hills.

Our destination was apparent from a considerable distance thanks to the sizeable spoil heaps. At about the same point the ruins of a large stone hut came into view in the bracken above.

'That's the explosives store,' explained David. 'They had to keep it a couple of hundred yards away from the mine itself on safety grounds.'

Five minutes later we were in front of a series of huge hillocks of dusty grey and brown sand. This fine powder was the detritus left after the ore had been crushed and its metals washed out. But there were lumpier piles above. Vic walked to these and picked up several stones. He showed them to me: 'See that grey colouring? That's lead,' he said. Then he pointed to a couple of small silvery pebbles embedded in the orange brown rock. 'And those little bits – they're tin.' He juggled the rocks up and down. 'Feel the weight of that – it's loaded with metals.'

'Just think,' he mused as he looked at the tonnes of ore, 'They must have come up here in early 1899 and dug all this out ready to be crushed and then one day the foreman turns round and says: 'That's it boys, we're out of here' and they just picked up their tools and walked out never to return.'

Vic sat down, took off his backpack and took out a white plastic cross about a foot in diameter. He deftly clipped a propeller blade to the end of each arm. This was his most important research tool – a state-of-the-art drone. He settled it on the ground and clipped his phone into a control box. After a moment's pause the cross whirred into life and lifted off, buzzing up into the blue skies before zig-zagging above the hillsides as Vic methodically photographed the mine with its shafts, spoil piles, forge and crushing works. The dogs lay on the dusty soil and panted.

Sheep were grazing on the hillsides opposite and – apart from the occasional buzzard, kite or raven – there were few signs of life in this deep cleft in the hills. The sun beat down and I stooped as we crossed the stream to return to the car to drink deeply from the cold water running off the hill.

'Steady on Dan!' said Dave. 'Haven't you seen all those sheep up there? There's three dead in the one mine shaft I looked at!'

Needless to say, I survived without the slightest problem and came off the hill in a gloriously wonderful mood.

And this area is riddled with long-lost mines which are usually short tunnels generally driven horizontally into the hillsides and still visible today. Mining has left its cultural mark too. Wales and Cornwall exchanged expertise through the centuries. Both men and skills were ferried back and forth across the Bristol Channel and many would have settled in their new homes, bringing families from home or marrying into the local community. Also, in the early days – seventeenth and eighteenth centuries – both Cornish and Welsh could have spoken falteringly to each other in their native tongues. Later, both provided sailors for the Antarctic whaling fleets, adding Celtic languages to what must have been a crowded on-board melting pot of cultures. And in the process they gave the world the Welsh and Cornish names for the great auk (pen gwyn or pedn gwydyn – white head) to the similar-looking flightless birds of the Southern Hemisphere.

Things start to break down when it gets to other raptors. A goshawk becomes a gwalch goch – literally 'red hawk' which sort of makes sense for a young bird still in its tawny immature plumage, but it fails lamentably when it comes to the blue-mantled three year-old adults. This epithet – gwalch glas – or blue hawk is reserved for the diminutive sparrowhawk, which is indeed blue in mature plumage, but surely this fails to do justice to this peppery little hedgerow hunter? The world's fastest living creature, the peregrine, is similarly dismissed as 'hebog glas' or blue falcon and the hen harrier is boda tynwen or – white bummed big bird.

It is true that English has the golden eagle, named after the adult's characteristic nape, but at least this is accurate. None of our other raptors are defined by colour and when it comes to the peregrine, the name is genuinely descriptive. The first mention is by a thirteenth century monk, Albertus Magnus, who mentions falco peregrinus. This refers to the falconry practice of trapping young migrating birds, for peregrinus means wanderer, traveller or stranger. This is what they naturally do for most of their early lives, thus Welsh peregrines can end up all over Britain – from the Severn Estuary to the Wash.

But to return to the Celtic links between Wales and Cornwall, I stumbled across another historical ornithological link on a working trip to the Ceredigion coast. While teaching media skills to a group of small businesses, I met Tim who had given up the rat race to run fishing safaris from New Quay. His specialism was fly fishing for bass from the rocky headlands – or, more of a challenge – from sea kayaks. I leaped at this and once again it seemed the perfect material for an article. We arranged to meet at Llangranog one morning. This pretty little former fishing village is found down an impossibly steep, narrow, valley. It has a small, but sandy beach at high tide, but as the sea retreats you can walk around a headland to a second, larger cove. Both are always crowded in good weather and on this occasion – a Saturday in late May – the sun was shining and sure enough the sand was covered with screaming children and dog walkers.

My heart sank – I don't like sharing my leisure time with crowds – but Tim just laughed: 'No, it's perfect,' he explained. 'People are so lazy they'll all stay here on the beaches which take no effort to reach. We're heading up there.' He pointed to steps cut into the headland to the north. We climbed up the stairs and sure enough, within five minutes were on our own, walking along the cliff top towards New Quay. There was a gentle breeze and plenty of birdsong coming out of the sea buckthorn on either side of the path. To our left we had the whole sweep of Cardigan Bay, its shallow waters azure in the early summer sunshine. At first the playful screams of children drifted up from Llangranog's second beach but we quickly left these behind.

After a few hundred yards we spotted half-a-dozen black birds foraging in a cow-grazed pasture. They were too small for crows, about jackdaw-sized, but they lacked the grey patch at the back of the head and when they wheeled into the air at our approach. They were supreme acrobats – in fact they made my local ravens look positively clumsy as they cavorted effortlessly in the invisible air currents above the cliffs, using the updrafts from the off-shore breeze and thermals from the warming sand below. After playing their aerial gymnastics for a while, they swung around to land some three hundred yards ahead. I unhooked the binoculars from my neck to study them. As we came closer I could see them in more detail. Most notable were the scarlet, delicately curved beaks which were designed to probe for insects under manure or in soft turf: the crow equivalent of a curlew.

These were choughs, the rarest of Britain's corvids. They congregate in small groups to search for insects in pastures and in many ways they are very similar to a seaside version of a jackdaw. They are teetering on the edge of extinction in Britain, but are fairly common around Cardigan Bay. To return to the links between Britain's two southerly Celtic nations, they are better known as the county bird of Cornwall and feature on the Prince of Wales's crest. Mind you, when I saw my small flock they had been absent from the West Country for half a century and most of Britain's two or three hundred pairs breed along Ceredigion cliffs, living mainly on insects found under cow pats and horse dung. A few years later I was to write an article for *Country Living* about an ancient breed of feral pony living on the Carneddau range in Western Snowdonia that received extra protection because of the dependence of local choughs on their dung piles.

Soon after I saw this small flock, the news reported a Welsh pair had recolonized Cornwall, giving credibility once more to Prince Charles's crest. And yet again it sent out natural ripples of the long-standing human ties between the Celtic peninsulas jutting out westwards from the rest of Britain and the Continent to the east.

We left the path a mile or so from Llangranog, to walk across a headland covered with thin close-cropped grass. It was pock-marked by rabbit burrows and halfway across there was an ancient wall, now no more than a foot high and mainly grass-covered, suggesting this had once been a warren where wild rabbits were contained and protected from predators while being ranched for food and pelts.

We walked across the turf although there were neither rabbits nor sheep in evidence – and then began to cut down a very steep path to the pebble-strewn beach below. The last part was such a scramble that a rope had been tied to a hook in the wall to allow the vaguely fit to scramble in relative safety to the shore. Although no more than a twenty minute walk from Llangrannog, we had the cove to ourselves.

To my mind this was the perfect beach. It had rock pools, sand, mussel-clad rocks, a couple of caves – and better still, no one else. Tim began to set up the rods, but declared flies were impractical because there was just too much wind. Instead he rigged up fake fish lures with triple hooks, each containing ball-bearings to make them rattle and shake in the water. This would attract the attention of the bass, voracious miniature versions of barracudas or sharks.

We cast and cast and cast, but there was no hint of a bite. After half an hour of biteless action, I don't have the patience and dedication of a natural fisherman, so was happy to give up to gather mussels, whelks and limpets from the rocks closest to the sea. This left Tim to continue casting happily from the rocks while I lit the camping stove to cook my haul. A pair of grey seals popped their heads out of the water to stare curiously at the intruders.

After quickly blanching the shellfish, I fried them in a knob of butter with a diced spring onion and garlic clove, finishing them off with a light steaming by covering them with seaweed. Meanwhile Tim seemed slighted by the failure to catch anything and was clearly on a mission: determined to prove it possible to catch fish from the shore. So he moved to the deeper water at the end of the beach. A peregrine floated overhead giving its loud kekk-ek-ekk call before drifting off downwind.

Tim kept casting and, a little later, gave a huge yell, reeling in a two-pound bass from his rocky promontory. Five minutes later he'd caught a second, yet despite this change in fortunes he dismantled his rod. He came back to join me cramming ocean-fresh shellfish into our mouths on rafts of fresh baguette. Salty juices from the mussels dribbled down our chins. It was the perfect end to the day. I'd like to say there was a peregrine overhead (there was), but sometimes just dribbling foraged juices sum it all up.

WATER

The Welsh coast is often overlooked by tourists in favour of the beaches of the South and West Country, but it has gems. The closest good beach to me is an hour away at Borth – a three-mile stretch of sand which stretches from the mouth of the Dovey almost as far as Aberystwyth. Although popular with locals, its sheer size means it is never crowded, not even in the height of summer, while in winter it is perfect for dog walking, hurling balls into the distance while watching the surf crash onto the sand as parasurfers hurtle across the waves. The beach has secrets too. A forest once grew here before the sea conquered it. Every few years a violent winter storm reveals the past, however, tearing away the sand to leave bare the petrified stumps and roots of the oaks that once covered the area.

But my favourite beaches are those that are just slightly off the beaten track or with awkward access. Pembrokeshire has a plethora of stunning beaches. Those with good parking – such as Broad Haven or Freshwater West – will have plenty of visitors, particularly in high summer, but the best are those which involve a walk of more than a few hundred yards. For example Marloes Sands in south west Pembrokeshire or the little cove of Pen Bryn in Ceredigion rarely have more than a handful of visitors, because access to each involves a ten minute walk and a significant descent.

The other coastal lure is the wildlife. Tim and Corinne have progressed from land-based bass fishing to boat-trips, taking small groups out of New Quay in pursuit of mackerel, pollock and dog fish. This is enjoyable, particularly for children, but for me the real lure is the animals. Gannets plummet like darts into the water, shearwaters live up to the name by skimming just above the surface while razorbills, guillemots and cormorants jostle on the cliffs.

Also there is always the chance of spotting something really unusual. A couple of years ago Cardigan Bay experienced an invasion of barrel jelly fish, each up to a metre across. They in turn are followed by predators. Once I caught sight of a huge fin sticking from the waves and turned in puzzlement to Tim: 'That's a sunfish!' he said with evident surprise and excitement. This strange-looking creature, with its disc of a body in front of a pair of two-metre long fins sticking vertically up and down, is normally found in the tropics, but it preys on jellyfish and follows them into the warm shallow waters off the Welsh coast. On another occasion I caught a brief glimpse of a rounded back protruding from the water. It was a leatherback turtle, another jellyfish-eater. Tim explained that although the was also rare, it was not unheard of – apparently the biggest leatherback ever found was a three-metre long monster washed up at Harlech.

However the real draw on these excursions are the dolphins. Sightings of these are far more reliable than wanderers from the Tropics. New Quay has a resident pod of about twenty bottlenoses which have become relatively immured to man. There are special boat trips which take large groups out to see them, but Tim and Corinne's expeditions are better – if anything there is more likelihood of seeing them up close from the quieter platform of a smaller boat. And one also always goes home with fresh fish for supper.

The coast is all very well, but my favourite swimming spot is not one of the glorious coves and beaches of Cardigan Bay. Instead it is a secluded bend of the Wye, a mile or two north of Rhayader. There is a natural pebble beach here, one which changes shape every year, due to the power of the winter floods. It has rocks, waterfalls and whirlpools and in many places is so deep I have never been able to touch the bottom – not even when jumping from a great height into the black depths.

The water is cold and dark on even the hottest of days, but always a magnet for children who dance in and out of the water. Generally it is too cold for me, so after a couple of plunges from the rocks into the washpool beneath the old railway bridge, I generally stalk the pebble beach with my camera, in search of the huge wolf spiders that are almost the size of my palm. They bask on the rocks, looking for prey until aware of my presence when they scuttle off to hide under the water-smoothed pebbles.

There are birds too. There is a peregrine eyrie nearby, one which has been used by countless generations of falcons for so long that it is apparently listed in the Domesday Book. If one approaches the river quietly – impossible with excited children - there is the chance of seeing dippers. These nest in rocky crevices and hunt caddisfly larvae by diving into the fast-flowing water. Sometimes I also catch the electric blue flash of a kingfisher flitting away downstream or a merganser, drawn by the plentiful minnows, trout and salmon par.

Once, while playing with a child's dipping net, I caught an unfamiliar writhing creature. At first I thought it was an eel, then a leech, but a closer look showed it was a lamprey. These are the most ancient of fish, devoid of jaws and instead armed with a circular set of tiny teeth. They spend their early lives in freshwater before moving into the sea until ready to return to breed. I don't know where they spawn locally, but I have watched the adults nesting on the river bed from a bridge some twenty miles downstream at Boughrood near Hay-on-Wye.

I was tipped off about their presence at the school gate by a neighbour, Caroline, who works for what was then the Countryside

Council for Wales. She had just been monitoring their numbers. It was a glorious June afternoon and she was flushed with pleasure at her morning's work. The next day after dropping the kids off at school I drove down to lean over the parapet. It was early summer and warm, with blue skies above and the clear waters of the Wye were silvered with reflected light. It took a few minutes to adjust my eyes, but sure enough after a while I spotted first one and then another and then another pair of arm-length fish in the gravel beds below. They hung there in the fast-flowing water, intertwining as the male lifted stones with his vacuum-like mouth to create a shallow bowl for his mate. When ready, she would shed her eggs into the trough for him to shake his milt into the surrounding water and then waft a thin layer of gravel over the precious future generation. The adults will only stay in the area for a week or two before they drift back to sea, but their young remain in the river for a year or so before they slip downstream to try life in the salt water of the Irish Sea or St George's Channel.

The youngsters begin life by feeding on microscopic organic matter floating downstream, but as they grow they become out-and-out parasites. Once they reach the sea, they change diet to latch onto the sides of bigger fish, boring through their scales and into flesh with their concentric rings of teeth. These resemble the mouths of the monstrous sand worms in the science fiction classic *Dune* or those of Jabba the Hutt's sand-dwelling pet monster, the Sarlacc, in *Revenge of the Jedi*.

Like many cartilaginous fish, their flesh is supposed to be soft and lacking texture, but they were once regarded as a delicacy. Thousands of lamprey teeth have been retrieved from the Viking latrines in York, while King John fined the City of Gloucester a small fortune for failing to produce his Christmas lamprey pie at the beginning of the thirteenth century. Most famously his great grandfather, Henry I, is supposed to have died of a 'surfeit of lampreys' on 1 December 1135.

Back at our watering hole, my musings on these ancient fish were interrupted by a sudden cry from the children. It has always struck me that growing up is a process of learning to anticipate. Children will play in snow, water or lie in the sun, only realising too late that they are cold or wet or too hot. Certainly our bathing trips invariably end when the first child realises he is nearing hypothermia. One by one the pale frames of the other children emerge to shiver, blue-lipped, from the dark swirl to be swathed in towels by the adults as they moan about the cold as is if it is some-one else's fault.

The river is too cold for swimming for most of the year – or at least it is too cold for most people and certainly for children. This doesn't mean it loses its attraction. Once, during some particularly hard weather I went to the swimming hollow to record it. In winter it is normally anything but a tranquil idyll, with huge volumes of foaming brown water charging down the valley, remoulding the pebble banks and sweeping branches and even trees downstream, to lodge briefly as they wedge between immovable huge rocks, only to be ripped loose again with the next downpour.

On this occasion, however, the usual thunderous winter torrent bellow was eerily absent. Instead there was a near total silence, the sound of traffic on the road above was muffled to a barely audible hum and even the falls, rapids and whirlpools seemed subdued. The water was still flowing over the rocks, but as soon as it levelled out, it shrank to nothing more than a jet black ribbon winding between two white sheets of ice.

The transformation from blissful family summers spent paddling, swimming and picnicking beneath blue skies and the monochrome embodiment of cold could not have been more stark, but as I took in the sight, my eye was caught by tracks on the snow-dusted ice leading upstream towards the falls. The two lines of left and right pad prints were separated a light line where a tail had just touched the snow. Closer inspection revealed the five-toed prints of an otter and, judging from the size, a bitch.

Freshwater has other attractions. There is something inherently peaceful about the placid surface of a lake or reservoir which makes them ideal for contemplation. On the hillside opposite the farm is a wood perched above a lake, Llyn Gwyn or 'white lake'. It is steeped in legend: the last resting place of Excalibur according to some, but that's a claim made for most lakes in Wales. Llyn Gwyn's recorded history says that it was certainly an important stew pond for nearby Abbey Cwmhir. The monks stocked it with alien carp imported from Central Europe in the early Middle Ages to provide food through Lent. Ironically, this tradition of stocking with non-native fish has continued in modern times, as the local angling association pours in hundreds of American rainbow trout every few months to augment the native browns. The rainbows have the advantage of being incapable of breeding in British waters so have no close season, allowing them to be fished all year.

The lake is also interesting in having no obvious inflow. Rainwater must obviously trickle down from the natural bowl of the hills, but there is no significant stream, brook or river feeding it with fresh water. Instead this deep natural lake is replenished by a subterranean inflow which bubbles up in its depths. Looking down towards the lake from my bedroom window, one can clearly see the scars on the landscape, the trenches gouged out by glaciers some ten thousand years ago. There is a clear line across the hillside which suggests a long-lost tide mark some fifty feet above the water level and above this is a large conifer plantation containing a mix of spruce and larch, with some more exotic large American conifers including Western hemlock and lodgepole pines.

Iolo Williams once told me that despite their secretive natures, goshawk nests are relatively easy to find: 'Just show me some forestry maps,' he once told me. 'There will be a pair in any decent-sized patch of conifers and the nest will almost certainly be in a larch about four or five rows in from the crossroads of two rides.' I thought this was possibly over-stating the case, but out of interest the next spring visited the wood on the opposite side of the valley at dawn. Sure enough I heard the loud and very distinctive kek-kek-kek calls of the male and when I walked up the hill spotted a large nest about twenty metres inside the wood near a big bend in the track.

This gave me an idea. I am not a natural fisherman – I don't have the patience to flick bits of feather and fluff over the water for hours on end – but the idea appeals. It is quiet and thoughtful and the fact that one doesn't catch anything is immaterial. It is also solitary and much as I like walking with friends in the countryside, sharing their observations, swapping information and admiring views, in the end nature is best observed in silence.

The knowledge there were goshawks nearby suggested early morning fishing trips at the lake could be productive in many ways, so I bought a seasonal licence and took up fishing. I caught very little, but it motivated me to visit the lake regularly. I would go at any time the sun was shining, but my favourite time was at dawn when I would bask in the warmth of the early sun while drinking in the sights, sounds and smells. I took to checking the forecast last thing at night and when things augured well, would get up next morning just as the skies to the east were starting to lighten. I would invariably have the waters to myself for the first hour or so and could clumsily flick my feathered hook out over the surface with no one to witness my ineptitude.

One morning about a fortnight after the summer solstice I was at the water's edge only a half an hour or so after dawn. The cluster of Scots pines on the bank cast long shadows over the water and there was a light mist on the water. It was easy to imagine a sword emerging magically from the depths. I unfurled the rod and fumbling in the light chill of morning, put an orange and black fly on the line and cast it out across the water. As usual I didn't really expect – or even hope – to catch anything, but it was the moment that mattered. After a few minutes I changed to a decidedly ugly fluffy white fly with a dash of fluorescent green fake fur and large bobbles next to the loop of the hook. These were supposed to resemble eyes. I much preferred some of the more genuinely fly-like versions in the box of secondhand flies I had bought from an ancient Rhayader angler who was hanging his rod up for good. In particular there was one with a rather stunning tiny red and black body and a delicate tuft of fine feather barbs sticking up from its back to resemble wings. But no, Tom who sells flies in the hardware shop and is one of the best of the younger generation of local anglers, assured me the cat's whiskers was the one that the Llyn Gwyn rainbows and browns would find irresistible.

Possibly they are irresistible when flicked over the water by a proficient angler, but nothing was rising as I cast again and again across the mirrored surface of the lake on this totally windless summer morning. It didn't matter. The scene was stunningly beautiful – blue skies with clouds still slightly pink from the sun which had only just risen behind the conifer-coated hill overlooking the lake. The mist was slowly dispersing, but the remnants were still gloriously romantic.

It was late in the breeding season, but there was still a semblance of a dawn chorus from those songbirds that were embarking on their second or even third clutches. Across the lake a pair of Canada geese cronked to each other as they launched from the dropping-strewn grass around their nest, encouraging their five goslings to follow. In the distance a tractor started up: probably intent on making the best of a good forecast to take in a crop of haylage after the shock of the previous harsh winter when everyone had run short.

And then I heard the thrilling clamour of young goshawks from the trees above the lake. It was faint, but unmistakeable. After a minute or two the volume increased and I waited with excitement, hoping against hope that the callers would break into the open. I knew, however, that this was unlikely because the hawks are wood-land hunters and are usually reluctant to leave the cover of the trees – at least not unless the air is warm and the valley bottoms are filled with those invisible aerial escalators: thermals. Also, judging from the plaintive note in the calls, I guessed these were almost certainly juveniles making their first tentative flights.

I was to be surprised, for about ten minutes later the first flew across the lake. It was difficult to be sure, but from its size it was a tiercel and this was confirmed a few moments later when first one and then another bigger juvenile female followed. Clearly the youngsters were starting to disperse. My hunch was that they were on a playful early flight – in theory hunting, but in practice testing each other out. They flew hard and fast – as is their wont – across the lake, calling to each other and giving begging calls to their parents (neither of which was evident). Had there been anyone else there, they would almost certainly have taken this as a family of buzzards, but these were the real McCoy, faster and with longer tails and more pointed wings.

This might have been a training flight in theory, but as true hawks they were also starting to hunt. Even at this age: maybe even more so, for at this age young hawks will take on almost anything, particularly when hungry. One bird ringer friend says he was at a property talking to the farmer when a spaniel burst out of the undergrowth with a juvenile female goshawk hanging on to the yelping dog's ears. This isn't quite as strange as it might sound. Young raptors can be triggered by movement and will attempt to catch prey that is far too big. They also tend to be 'sticky-footed', a falconry term which describes the way that their feet can lock tight on prey and the hawk, pumped up with hormones, is unable to release the tension. Thus the goshawk going for a Nantucket sleigh ride on the spaniel probably had little option but to ride the terrified dog. Similarly, one of the biggest causes of young osprey mortality is drowning after they seize a fish too big to lift from the water.

The three goshawks flew straight across the lake and disappeared into the scrub by the entrance to the lake. This was potentially good hunting ground, for the first broods of young grey squirrels and magpies would be around, each a relatively easy catch for even an eyass. It was one of the most memorable natural history sightings I've ever made – probably only reinforced by the fact that despite returning to the lake several times during the next week, I didn't see the young birds again and despite straining my ears, I failed to catch even a peep of a call.

FARMING LANDSCAPE

The Cambrians are ancient and bear the scars of our ancestors. One needs to look carefully. Although generally known as 'drovers' roads' most date back to Neolithic days. There are the unpaved pathways across grass, rarely walked today, but still traceable due to the scars left by first the feet of early man and then the hooves of countless cattle and sheep are scored into the hills.

Many of the earliest recorded paths were those made by early Christian missionaries in the Dark Ages. Indeed, the most famous local track is called the Monks' Trod. Today it runs between two tiny villages, each in the middle of nowhere, but once it connected the two great Cistercian abbeys of Strata Florida to the east of Aberystwyth and Abbey Cwmhir six miles north of Llandrindod Wells. These two great buildings fell into disrepair and ruin after the dissolution of the monasteries, but these and other paths continued to be used by generations of drovers driving their herds and flocks to the richer markets of the Midlands. Sometimes these traces of the past are little more than soil which has been too tightly compacted for years of encroaching bracken to swallow completely, in other cases a remote bridge or ford bears testimony to past traffic. The knowledgeable will also note a small group of Scots pines next to an isolated homestead in the hills. This was a primitive pub sign for the illiterate and mapless herdsmen. It meant a fold for the livestock was on hand and the drover could expect a bed and a simple meal.

The need to pay their way on the two or three week journey meant drovers had to travel with plenty of cash to pay for their passage: robberies and even murders were frequent. So they developed a large and independent breed of dog – the cŵn coch, the 'red dog', but known in English as the Welsh sheepdog – a bigger, often rusty-coloured, version of the more familiar black and white border collie most people know from *One Man and His Dog*. The latter work closely with the shepherd, obeying commands to the letter. The cŵn coch were developed to herd independently, ranging far afield to bring back stragglers under their own initiative. Just as importantly they needed to be more aggressive for they had to protect their drover masters from vagabonds along the route.

While the advent of the railways nearly two centuries ago fatally undermined the droving way of life, the Scots pines and the scars of the trampling hooves through the thin topsoil are still visible if one looks carefully. Many converge at towns like Llanidloes, Rhayader or Builth, for the livestock would have to cross either the Wye or the Severn on their way from the fertile pastures of Ceredigion to the wealthy towns and cities of the Midlands. Thus while to the modern traveller all three towns are comparatively insignificant, for many centuries the three played vital economic roles out of all proportion to their sizes. They were central hubs for travellers.

Rhayader is the last readily fordable point on the Wye for much of the year and the existence of a free crossing point gave the town a strategic importance out of all proportion to its size. Today its population is barely one thousand strong, but during the turbulent Middle Ages it boasted a garrisoned castle and the church graveyard still contains a mass grave – testament to an outbreak of plague which killed half its garrison. Later drovers from Ceredigion would pause here after crossing the Cambrians to rest their flocks in Cwmdauddwr's meadows and drink in the pubs (when I arrived in 1993 the town had thirteen drinking holes, one for every eighty inhabitants).

There are other largely forgotten, but once economically vital, drovers' roads in the locality. One just to the south connected Tregaron and Abergwesyn to Builth and Hereford. A little to the north there were paths leading from Aberystwyth to Llanidloes and then on to Shrewsbury, while a network of lesser routes connected towns such as Knighton, Presteigne and Kington to Hereford. Some of these have been transformed with tar and paint into modern roads, but most have gently subsided into the landscape and are barely visible today.

The transport importance of these roads to the local economy was illustrated dramatically during the 1840s when, briefly, Rhayader became a hotbed of radicalism and revolt. At the same time as the great industrial towns were rocked by the political Chartist movement, in rural Wales it was the increasing cost of travel which was making the population restless. The cost of road main-tenance was ostensibly met by levying tolls at gates set across the main roads. These were levied by private trusts or, in some cases the Church in Wales, and had never been popular. A deep agricultural recession in the late 1830s and a marked rise in toll charges bought matters to a head and to make things even worse, many trusts put up 'trap' gates on lanes used by locals to by-pass the main gates.

The first popular protests broke out in Carmarthenshire in 1839 when a crowd tore down a new 'trap' gate. To disguise themselves, many of the men adopted an old protest tradition by dressing as women and blacking their faces. The unrest spread north along the Cambrians and arrived in Rhayader in late 1843. There were six gates controlling movements in and out of the town. Two were pulled down in late October and the remaining four were destroyed by armed rioters a fortnight later. This proved to be the last of the riots: the government, thoroughly alarmed, set up a commission which was eventually to lead to the end of the toll road system.

The drovers were also consigned to history as the Victorian mania for railway building made it far cheaper and quicker to send livestock to market by train. By the 1860s droving was as good as dead, although to a degree it lived on in Rhayader. The first farm in the area to get mains electricity was on the outskirts of the town. The farmer had grazing rights in the Elan Valley and for years he would drive some 3000 ewes down through the town to be mechanically sheared. To this day there is no mains power in the Valley, but portable diesel generators have been available for years and for half a century the sheep drive continued simply because it was 'traditional'.

It could take up to an hour for the sheep to flow through the town, completely halting traffic in the process. The threat of fisticuffs from irate lorry drivers was ever-present with the result the police had to turn out to supervise the event. Eventually the drive had to stop during the foot-and-mouth outbreak, thus demonstrating that local agriculture could cope perfectly well without disrupting life for scores of innocent travellers. Thus with an almost audible sigh of relief the police put a stop to the spurious practice after that.

The disused drovers' roads snaking across the landscape may be many centuries old, but they are modern in comparison to the tumbled stone structures dotted along the valley ridges to the west of Tan y Cefn. They are just visible from the decking at the end of the barn as slight bumps on the horizon and for years I looked at them with mild curiosity, vowing one day to investigate. It took me twenty years to fulfil this promise to myself but when I finally did walk around the tops of this glacial bowl I was rewarded with spectacular views south to the distant Brecon Beacons.

The stone structures were a puzzle however. A dozen of these rock piles are strung out along the ridge, but their purpose escaped me. My first thought was that they might be enclosures for livestock, but they were on exposed hilltops, not in the shelter of the valley bottom. I wondered if they might be butts, for there are still a few red grouse in the area and in the Victorian era there might well have been just enough for shooting. But again the positioning seemed wrong – they were too high and too far apart. In the end I asked a local historian and was told they are Neolithic burial cairns. Apparently this is the biggest concentration of five thousand year-old graves anywhere in Europe.

Another local legend is that Llyn Gwyn, the 'white lake' at the bottom of my valley is the last resting place of Excalibur and while Wales is dotted with lakes making the same claim, there is something mystical about the place in early morning when the one of the frequent spring or autumnal mists drifts over the water. The place can be eerily silent too – disturbed only by the slurp and ripples of a carp feeding in the muddy shallows and the honks of the Canada geese gathered on their favourite grassy bank.

There are other Arthurian connections. Some say Camlo Hill behind Nantmel gets its name from a corruption of Camelot. This is contested by others who believe nearby Castle Hill is the real site of the king's court. According to some, Arthur's uncle was Vortigern, King of the Britons, who fled to Mid-Wales after making the disastrous mistake of inviting the Danes and Saxons to cross the Channel. He alternately fought and made peace with the invaders until, eventually, his exasperated courtiers assassinated him at Bwlch Llys ('sheltered pass'). The present house is a relatively recent Victorian construction of dressed stone, but like all the farms it was built on the site of a succession of previous homesteads. It nestles on the hill behind Tan y Cefn just a five minute walk across the fields, but five miles by road. This is yet another highly dubious myth, but a genuine Dark Ages treasure horde was discovered on the same hill in the early twentieth century by a local farmer hunting foxes on its boulder-strewn slopes. It was quickly dubbed 'Vortigern's gold' and is now on display in Cardiff Museum.

WELSH RAPTORS

My urge to move to Wales had been driven by the knowledge that I would be living surrounded by most of Britain's two dozen raptors. From the start I was not disappointed. The buzzards were plentiful enough, but for the first two or three years a pair of kestrels nested in a row of pines two hundred metres in front of the house. The nesting parents would be unobtrusive, but evident, from spring onwards, flying in and out of the tree where they had taken over an old crow's nest about twenty feet below the crown. The family became much more evident for a week or two after the young had fledged and would hone their flying skills around the nest site, crying and half-heartedly chasing each other.

One day, I was watching the fledglings as they circled above their nest tree when suddenly one broke off and headed straight towards me. Three or four seconds later it was followed by first one, then a second and then the last sibling. They flew directly towards the house and then continued in a dead straight line to fly overhead towards the hilltop. What their intended destination might have been, I have no idea, but they were clearly intent on crossing the hill towards Rhayader.

Ironically, although the general public associates falconry with aristocracy and privilege, today its strongholds are in former industrial areas: especially those with particular ties to mining. The great Ken Loach film, *Kes*, based on the Barry Hines book *A Kestrel for a Knave*, charts the link between working class Billy and a wild-caught falcon. Hines based the story on his brother's experiences training hawks and South Yorkshire is another bastion of the sport. The same connection between tough industrial working men and predators is also very strong in South Wales, even though the mines and almost all the steel have long gone.

My obsession with hawks had begun with an injured kestrel and while I only had it for three weeks, the seed was sown and for the next twenty years I read and re-read every falconry book I could find. As the only significant literary work, *The Goshawk* by T.H. White made the most impact, but I also devoured every manual I could find. Most were old and based around the four 'classic' European species: merlin, peregrine, sparrowhawk and goshawk. Unfortunately, all of these were effectively impossible to obtain: the first three being particularly hard hit by DDT and the last effectively extinct in Britain.

Thus a sustainable wild harvest in raptors which had existed for thousands of years across the world dried up completely in Britain in the 1970s. This appeared a disaster to most traditionalists, but it actually had unexpected benefits, mainly because it gave a real impetus to captive-breeding which until then had been assumed to be near-impossible. As captive-bred hawks – particularly those derived from imports such as harris hawks, red tails, sakers and lanners – became increasingly available, so prices began to fall and hawk keeping became far more widespread, particularly in the former coal fields.

When I finally managed to take up the sport as an adult, it was to start with a red-tailed buzzard, an American bird which has been described as a 'turbo-charged' European buzzard. Later I got a succession of harrises, another bird from the Americas, but while they are great fun to fly, particularly in a 'cast' (pair), I find them ugly. I wanted to fly a native bird in a Welsh landscape, thus I found myself dreaming of acquiring a goshawk – preferably a large female

– but was put off by the high price and their reputation for being 'difficult'.

I should say that although the word falconry is used loosely to describe anyone who flies a trained bird of prey, it actually has two branches. There is 'true' falconry which involves flying long-winged members of the Falco family. These are highly aerial and most specialise in catching other birds. The pinnacle of the sport today would be to fly peregrines at grouse or merlins at skylarks, but in the past the quarry would also have included herons and red kites. This form of hunting is inefficient and requires large areas of open country, horses to follow the flight and, usually, a large entourage to help recover the hawk. Not surprisingly it was rightly regarded as a sport for the rich.

The other branch uses hawks, ambush specialists which hunt their prey in short sprinting flights. While modern hawkers (or austringers, to give them their traditional name) are most likely to use a harris or red tail, in the past the goshawks and sparrowhawks were the mainstay. These are accomplished killers and the falconer is far more likely to return home with plenty of edible game in his bag than the moorland hunter with his peregrine. Indeed, the goshawk was known as 'the cook's hawk' for its prowess in bringing both fur and feather to book.

This was the species that I had always hankered after: stunningly good-looking birds which in adult plumage have blue-grey backs with a white and black-barred breast. The eyes are also impressive – yellow in youth, but slowly turning orange and even red as they age.

They also have an interesting history in Britain. They are a genuinely native species, present here since at least the last Ice Age and were harvested by falconers since at least the age of Vortigern. Unfortunately goshawks do not mix well with pheasants and when game shooting took off in the early nineteenth century, their days were numbered. Any determined gamekeeper with time and fieldcraft would have been able to exterminate hawks on his patch without too much difficulty. Guns at the nest site, pole traps on suitable vantage points and poisoned baits on plucking posts would quickly account for even this shyest of predators. The hawks' problems were compounded by the Victorian passion for stuffed animals and the rarer the creature, the more it appealed to the taxidermist. The last great two auks were killed on St Kilda in 1840 for their bodies, for example, while goshawks were extinct a few years later and by the First World War ospreys and sea eagles had gone too.

They were to return, however. Falconers discovered they could import goshawks from German and Swedish gamekeepers who would otherwise destroy nests on their patches. In the days before radio tracking, these were extremely easy to lose and many went feral. But others were given positive help. Helen MacDonald in *H is for Hawk* suggests it was barely more expensive to get a keeper to send two birds from a clutch rather than one. So many falconers would import a pair, either to release one deliberately or to cover themselves for accidental loss.

Some of this was deliberately cavalier: until at least the 1970s goshawks were thought impossible to breed in captivity, not least because the females had an alarming tendency to kill and eat their smaller mates. The ambition of many mid-twentieth century falconers was to re-establish a wild breeding population that might – in due course – be harvested under licence. Thus there was a steady stream of deliberate and accidental releases during the sixties, but it wasn't until about 1970 that the full impact of the DDT crisis became clear. This released a tsunami in environmental attitudes towards hawks. Until the middle of the century most people regarded them as pests. There was an officially-sanctioned campaign to kill peregrines during the war because of the threat they posed to carrier pigeons and estate owners encouraged their keepers to shoot buzzards, sparrowhawks and harriers on sight. it wasn't until the 1950s that any raptor received a modicum of legal protection. This was to change a decade later when the populations of almost all British birds of prey plummeted. The problem had come from the organophosphates used by farmers to control insects. These long-lasting chemicals worked their way up the food chain to be concentrated at the top of the pyramid. Their worst effect was to build up in the birds' oviducts where they impeded calcium release. This weakened eggs to the point that the shells would collapse under the weight of the incubating parent. Populations of all raptors, but particularly bird-eaters such as peregrines and sparrowhawks, crashed.

Environmental catastrophes have a galvanising effect on the British public. Today we focus on climate change and plastic, but fifty years ago it was pesticides. Legal protection was ratcheted up and the licensing system which allowed falconers to take birds from the wild was wound up. This had unexpected side effects. One was to give a huge impetus to captive-breeding to fill the vacuum created by the end of the wild-take, but it also prompted some people to mount private reintroduction schemes in the hope that in due course the licensing scheme would restart.

There is a particular Welsh connection here. One of the most enthusiastic goshawk releasers – and one of the few that admits he deliberately released a score of hawks – is based near Carmarthen. This area is ideal goshawk territory, thanks in large part to the huge pine plantations stretching north along the Cambrians. These woodland hunters have a particular fondness for squirrels, crows and pigeons all of which abound in the conifers, but which have few human friends. As a result the Forestry Commission, owners of the woods, was pleased by the new arrivals. Indeed their presence was trumpeted by its press office because the large blocks of dense alien subsidised conifers were seen as ecological deserts that had few benefits for native wildlife. Just as significantly there are few shooting interests in Wales, so the presence of such a clear threat to pheasants prompted little persecution. They have certainly thrived here and are now found across Wales. In fact, the Principality is probably home to more than half of Britain's now thriving goshawk population – although precise figures are impossible to pin down. The best guess for goshawks is that there are at least a thousand pairs in total, more than half of which are in Wales.

It was Iolo Williams who showed me my first goshawk. It was on our trip up to North Wales and as we walked along a ride through a dense conifer plantation he suddenly pointed up at a large bird crossing from left to right above us: 'Female goshawk,' he said simply. 'You can tell from the pigeon chest.' I'd seen it too fleetingly to see more than a fast-moving buzzard-sized bird, but from what Iolo told me, I was sure there must be a healthy local population. On several occasions I saw soaring buzzards that didn't 'look quite right', with tails which seemed a bit too long and wings that were slightly too tapered. The other suspicious factor was speed – some seemed to be moving far more quickly than the normal buzzard with its classic three wing beats; glide; three wing beats; glide, but I could never trust my suspicions, knowing how much I wanted it to be this falconry icon. Yet I always knew there must be a resident goshawk population and the sight of the young goshawks flying across the lake breathed new life into that smouldering fuse in my imagination.

When I first took up falconry as a sport, goshawks were difficult and expensive to acquire. Things change, however, and twenty years later it suddenly became apparent that breeders were now producing sufficient numbers for prices to have dropped sharply. The year after I had seen the three youngsters I was left a small legacy by a godmother. She had also loved *The Goshawk* so I was sure she would have approved of my investing the money to fulfil a childhood dream.

I was apprehensive for the hawks have a reputation for being difficult and temperamental, but to my surprise Sky was anything but tricky. Indeed she soon proved herself to be a pure delight to train and fly. This came as a surprise until I stumbled across a new falconry book where the author suggested their reputation is largely down to White's description of his cack-handed attempts at training a wild-caught tiercel in the late 1930s. Sky, on the other hand, was one of the easiest birds I've ever trained. Indeed, once I was flying her free, she soon proved to have a wonderful, dog-like, desire to re-join me after a failed flight.

A large part of this is because she's been imprinted – in other words carefully brought up not by another hawk, but reared in close proximity to man for a few critical weeks just before fledging. The chick sits in a large tank or mesh pen, able to see people, dogs and vehicles – anything with which it should be comfortable with in later life. The one critical point is that between three and ten weeks, it must not associate man with food. If it does, the benefits of being reared as part of the family are completely undone, for it associates humans with food. This stimulates a parental relationship and it triggers 'begging behaviour' – roughly akin to transforming it into the worst perpetual human teenager. It can become extremely aggressive towards the falconer as well as screaming on the fist with a peculiarly penetrating shriek only inches from the ear. But when well done, the hawk merely familiarises itself with things that could send a parent-reared hawk into paroxysms and, in theory, becomes 'bomb-proof'. This is good for the hawk because it reduces stress (which can lead to becoming prone to various diseases), but more importantly it creates a bird which is much calmer and more comfortable in the presence of humans and it is also good for breeding purposes. Hawk reproduction in the confines of a relatively small breeding chamber can be a risky process for the smaller males, with the females' hunting instincts all too often triggered by injudicious behaviour by her mate. Imprinting means both male and female hawks are sexually attracted to humans which allows the falconer to collect semen from the one and then to 'mate' with the female.

On the other hand, sex is a powerful force and a goshawk that is pumped up with oestrogen can be quite a handful, often becoming very violent towards her potential mate - in this case me. The early warning signs come in late winter. When excited, particularly after a hunt, Sky would land on my glove, gripping tightly and massaging my thumb and finger, Do I mean 'massaging'? She exerts huge power through those feet and can be incapable of letting go as I try to weigh her. For most of the year I would happily have her on my bare hand – I trust her completely – but now she's really fired up and every time she detects the slightest movement between her claws she wriggles them back and forth, exerting massive pressure. Were my hand to be unguarded, they would easily go straight through the palm.

The first signs of a real desire to mate are when she starts to 'raise her petticoats', dipping her head and raising her tail to show off the fluffy white under-feathers around her vent. She also bends down on the fist to nibble the glove or my finger. But these displays of affection are perilously close to aggression and early in the breeding season she is easily prone to lash out with her feet which are tipped with eight needle-sharp nails and the slightest contact almost invariably draws blood. As behoves a top predator, she is lightening fast and if she is in a footing mood it is almost impossible to avoid blood loss. Worse, this all too often goes septic thanks to the rich bacterial soup between the ridges on the underside. As I started my latest course of antibiotics (my doctor now writes a prescription for collection if I merely phone up for 'the usual'), it struck me that the mortality rate from septicaemia among falconers must have been high in pre-penicillin days.

There are many reasons to be entranced by birds of prey, but one of the less trumpeted is the way the hawk's incredible powers of sight add to the way one sees the countryside. Or to be more precise the hawk sees things that one doesn't or in many cases simply can't. On one occasion for example I walked up the hill behind the house in late summer. This is open country, with no trees. To fly a hawk lower down the valley is to invite trouble because the hawk inevitably lands in a tree and is instantly invisible amongst the foliage.

So instead I trudged up the steep slope to get a view of Rhayader as the sun started to dip in the west. As with most local hills, the steep slopes smooth out to form a plateau and as we trudged across this, the hawk suddenly stiffened and then burst off my fist. She flew low and fast across the field, clearly with something in her sights. She covered four hundred metres in a matter of seconds before powering into a clump of marsh grass. There was a commotion in the undergrowth and a hare careered out of the other side. The hawk took off after it and put in two more attacking passes before giving up, almost out of sight. With heart in mouth I began to run towards the point where I had last seen her. I was manically whistling and waving the lure and to my surprise she was in the air a few seconds later to power back towards me. The safe recovery of a hawk after even a temporary disappearance always leaves me glowing with a sense of relief and my mood as I returned home was further enhanced by a spectacular sunset.

BACK FROM THE DEAD

Autumn is a general time of plenty and this in turn gives wonderful wildlife watching opportunities. The fields, hedgerows and woods are full of food and birds, mammals and even invertebrates are desperate to stock up for the coming colder months. To make things even better for the wildlife watcher, many of the creatures scouring the land for calories are youngsters, creatures that are relatively unversed in risks and so more easily observed.

The chances are greatly improved with modern technology such as trail cameras. These small, waterproof, digital cameras are set up in the woods or fields and activated by sensors which detect movement. I installed one by our pond and left if for a week before downloading the images. There were many creatures on there. Foxes, badgers and rats were all predictable, but there were others that were much less so. A couple of polecats appeared, as did a muntjac (these are common in nearby Herefordshire, but rare here).

But the species I secretly hoped to find was the pine marten. This arboreal weasel is a Welsh enigma. Does it exist as a native? A beautiful lithe hunter, it was once found all over Britain, but was slowly exterminated across England during the nineteenth century. By the early twentieth century it was confined to pockets in Scotland and Wales, plus perhaps, northern parts of the Pennines and Lake District.

When I arrived at Tan y Cefn it was absent from England and so rare in Wales that there was an intensive search to establish whether any remained. The last definitive proof came from the

1970s, but although there were regular sightings from credible witnesses after that, there was no concrete proof in the form of a corpse, fur or droppings. That said, I was told the most credible reports came from a broad arc sweeping up and around from Carmarthen in the south west through Llandovery, Builth and across to Knighton. John Messenger of the Vincent Wildlife Trust, the man charged with collating these sightings, told me three of the most detailed sightings came from a farmer in our valley.

One reason he was so anxious to establish the truth was linked to reintroduction. Several groups were keen to see them brought back to the Principality, but environmental politics are complex. One fundamental is that you shouldn't introduce new genes from outside an area which might dilute the 'pure native' stock. Thus if there is a small residual population of Welsh pine martens, it could be detrimental to bring in Scottish animals.

And then we come to another problem which, were it to be applied to humans, would be deeply racist and utterly unacceptable. Some ecologists argue there are at least two strains of pine marten. Scottish animals are more omnivorous and a little less arboreal than the – possibly extinct – Welsh version. However the latter strain was probably introduced to Ireland by monks a millennia ago in a fur ranching exercise and its descendants are thriving in places such as the Burren on the West Coast. As a result some of the purists who want to see a reintroduction to Wales, were actually strongly against translocating Scottish animals, arguing stock should be sourced from Ireland instead. These animals would be more genetically 'pure' in Welsh terms, goes the argument.

Such discussions hamstrung the higher echelons of the conservation movement for some time, but with no evidence of a surviving Welsh population, the arguments of the purists dwindled. By the early years of this century the idea looked increasingly possible and – ironically – the discovery of a pine marten corpse on a road near Newtown in Mid-Wales actually spurred things on. Genetic analysis suggested this was European in origin which suggested a freewheeling eco-individual or group was conducting their own private release programme.

This is not so far-fetched. There is circumstantial evidence that well-intentioned conservationists are quietly by-passing the official restrictions on reintroductions to right the wrongs of the past. For example, wild boar were exterminated in Britain in the late Middle Ages. They returned in agricultural diversification schemes as farmed animals in the 1980s, but some escaped in Kent. These thrived and further farm escapes saw them living free in one or two other spots along the south coast. They were few in number, localised but clearly breeding.

In the early years of this century, however, around fifty turned up overnight on the Welsh Marches in the Forest of Dean. For about a month this huge 'sounder' was very visible and relatively easy to approach, much to the amazement, concern and alarm of local people. It was clear from their sudden arrival and initial tameness that they were captive-bred, but even so, these would have been only a few generations removed from their wild forebears. Not surprisingly they reverted as rapidly to their instincts as would a goshawk or peregrine.

Within a couple of months they had become reclusive and the huge herd had broken up into the small matriarchal groups that are typical of their wild ancestors. They melted into the Forest and for a few years almost vanished apart from occasional encounters with dog walkers. They thrived however and there are now thought to be several thousand living there. Pressure of numbers has even meant they are spreading out – there have been numerous sighting north of the Wye near Monmouth – so it seems Wales has regained a long-lost resident. They are almost certain to take off as a species here given the perfect mix of woodland and pastoral habitats, plus the total absence of predators.

But where did these Gloucestershire boar come from? Their sudden appearance in a prime habitat can only point to a deliberate human release. Quite why is more ponderable. None of the handful of highly-regulated British farms had reported escapes. This leaves a deliberate, but illegal, release from either a failing wild boar farm or by a private re-wilding scheme. The last is more likely than one might imagine. There are several high-profile enthusiasts who back the reintroduction of lost creatures (usually iconic predators such as wolves or lynx), but no doubt there are lot more that fly beneath the radar.

Were I a rich individual intent on a reintroduction, I might well take one look at the red tape and near-insuperable official barriers, eschew publicity, and quietly release without recognition. It looks as if this has happened more than once with boar for isolated pockets of the animals have cropped up many miles from the two or three known escapes from farms in the Weald and Dorset.

Whatever the motives, boar are here and clearly thriving. Most people welcome this with almost as much gusto as I have cheered the return of the goshawk. The way things are going it is not improbable that I will see a boar in a Radnorshire wood before I die, but not everyone will share this sentiment. Wild pigs can be incredibly destructive and they carry livestock disease too. They also have no natural predators, so any form of control has to be with extremely high-powered rifles – not things which are welcome in a densely-populated nation with concerns about terrorism.

Boar certainly have right to claim residency. They were common in Wales until the Middle Ages and feature in Arthurian myth. One legend concerns a giant wild boar, Twrch Trwyth. A Welsh prince, Culhwch, fell madly in love with a giant's daughter, Olwen. When he asked her father for her hand, he was set a series of impossible tasks, one of which was to retrieve the magical comb, razor and scissors which the huge beast kept hidden in the bristles behind his ear.

Culhwch went to negotiate with the boar, but his pleas fell on deaf ears, so the desperate prince asked his cousin Arthur and his warriors for help. The king and his knights hunted Trwyth and his seven piglets back and forth across Wales, leaving a record of the hunt in place names along the way, one of which, Carn Gafallt (Gafallt's Cairn), is a stone on top of a local hill and named after Arthur's favourite hunting dog which was killed there by the boar. One by one the young boar were finished off and eventually Trwyth was chased into the sea and drowned.

To return to present day realities, however, the discovery of the road casualty marten finally kick-started a reintroduction pro-gramme. To be precise this was labelled a 'reinforcement programme' for the official line is that Welsh animals still exist but in such low numbers that they are vulnerable to extinction. Thus between 2015 and 2017 some fifty Scottish martens were released around Devil's Bridge. These were carefully monitored, some with radio-tracking, and they appear to be thriving, with evidence of breeding and a range that is spreading significantly.

The release site is only fifteen miles or so from Tan y Cefn. It was picked not only because the habitat around there is ideal, but over the past twenty years many of the most plausible sightings of genuine Welsh martens have been from around here. Thus I live in hope that the trail camera mounted in the wood by my pond will reveal the pointed face and distinctive creamy throat bib of this beautiful hunter.

This is not the only reintroduction scheme. The last Welsh beaver was killed in the mid-fifteenth century, probably somewhere high in the Cambrians. A few years later it was followed by the last wolf, which was hunted down in the early years of the Tudors. Several places claim the dubious honour of the site of the final kill: the tiny hamlet of Bleddfa, 'the place of the wolf', near Knighton is one, although a village a few miles outside Carmarthen is another claimant.

Despite various loudly-trumpeted schemes to reintroduce wolves, there seems no real chance of their return to a sheep-filled countryside, but beavers are another matter. For the past decade there has been a well-funded reintroduction project, backed by European environmental legislation and several respected conservation bodies. Yet despite this and several announcements of imminent releases, beavers have yet to be launched into the wild. This is testimony to the difficulties of bringing back a creature which has been missing from the countryside for many centuries. Over time new vested interests have built up. In the case of beavers the biggest problems come from anglers who fear the impact of their dams on migratory fish such as salmon and sewin. Although science suggests this is not a genuine problem (many of Scandinavia's greatest salmon rivers have resident beavers), conservation politics are delicate and so far cautious diplomacy seems to rule the roost.

Eagles are also possible reintroduction candidates. I mentioned this to Iolo Williams on one of our early journalistic trips as we talked about reintroduction schemes. I observed the Welsh for Snowdonia, Eryri, is supposed to mean 'Land of Eagles'. Iolo politely ignored this patronising comment (he was, after all, born in eastern Snowdonia and raised with Welsh as his first language) but his response really surprised me.

'I certainly hope they don't!' he said. 'It would be a disaster!'

I was quite shocked, for he clearly loved his raptors. 'Why?'

'Well, for a start I don't think there's enough food or territory out there to sustain a viable population,' he explained. 'They may do all right in Scotland, but there are plenty of rabbits, mountain hares, moorland game birds and deer,' he went on. 'But in Wales these are largely or completely missing.' The real problem, he went on, was the sheer size of these powerful birds with their six-foot wingspans and feet the size of a human hand, armed with two inch talons and with enough strength to drive these stilettos through the chest of a fox or roe deer.

'It has taken the RSPB half a century to persuade Welsh farmers that buzzards don't kill lambs and to stop putting out poisoned baits,' he said. 'We've succeeded and there is very little poisoning here now, but can you imagine what would happen if we had a large buzzard-looking bird that is definitely capable not only of killing a lamb, but flying off with it? We'd be facing a huge outbreak of poisoning all over their range ... and beyond.'

I was disappointed, but his comments were backed up some years later in a conversation with a very senior official from the then Countryside Council for Wales. I mentioned reintroducing eagles and to my slight surprise he said they had been actively looking at the idea, only to dismiss it.

'Unfortunately our studies say there simply isn't the habitat,' he said. 'Snowdonia and the Cambrians may seem to be huge areas of wilderness, but a pair of eagles really does need a very large territory and in addition, most of the hills are heavily grazed. Even if there were room for one or two pairs, that wouldn't be a genetically viable population.' He conceded, however, that the even larger, but more scavenging and coastal white tailed sea eagle might be a more viable option.

So with a mild sense of sorrow, I put the idea of Welsh eagles to the back of my mind until about five years ago when I began to hear stories of eagle sightings in the Tregaron area. At first I dismissed the tales, but then Tom, a credible birder, told me he'd definitely seen a huge raptor, although he said it didn't 'look quite right'. I made enquiries among falconry friends and it soon emerged that an eagle keeper with a distinctly cavalier attitude towards flying his birds free, had lost a tawny/golden hybrid just south east of the 'Town on the Bog'.

He lived only a few miles from the vast wet wilderness from which the town gets its name and above which there are hundreds of square miles of uninhabited Welsh mountainsides, patrolled over solely by hefted sheep – which have a high natural mortality. It wasn't difficult to imagine that a solitary scavenging eagle might have been able to eke out an existence in the hills, largely unobserved and troubling no one. However after a while the sightings ceased and that seemed to be the end of things.

That was until spring 2019, when there was a story on the news about a Cardiff University scheme to release golden eagles in Snowdonia. I sat up in bed abruptly when I heard this and listened attentively for the story to be explained. My heart naturally leaped, but there was very little detail. So I resorted to Google and quickly established that once more poor journalism was at fault. The editors, looking for a sensationalist twist, had leaped on an interesting bit of research and turned what was effectively a theory into a reality. At this stage the academics are merely surveying possible release areas to establish whether the project is viable: in other words, how many pairs might Wales be able to sustain? Would they cause any problems? And what would be the popular reaction to the sudden appearance of these such large and potentially destructive predators? There certainly was no suggestion of an imminent release.

This echoes the constantly repeated stories that lynx and wolves are about to return to our shores. When examined in detail, the lurid stories of large predators about to be patrolling our fields and woods always stem from the enthusiastic amateur backers of such schemes. They certainly lack the necessary support from licencing authorities, let alone the vital backing of landowners and farmers. They are akin to the announcement of a 'cancer pill' which actually turns out to be someone making a minor but potentially promising discovery in cell structures.

All the same, the concept of eagles flying free over Wales is far more viable than releasing large cats or wolves in a small island full of livestock. And as if to give it extra weight, the vestigial eagle population (two pairs) in Galloway is being boosted by translocated Highland birds with the full blessing of local landowners. There the benefit to eco-tourism has been taken on board and given the success of Welsh kite-feeding stations over the past couple of decades, it could well be that Iolo's dire predictions of the 1990s are now outdated. I certainly hope so. Whilst as a falconer I know there is very little potential wild food in the Cambrians for a bird the size of an eagle, they are built to patrol over thousands of acres of desolate uplands. They hunt either by waiting patiently on a cliff for something to move in the valley below (and they can see a rabbit at well over a mile), or to cruise at an altitude of several thousand feet and they also readily take carrion. There is plenty of this in the form of fallen stock, although there would be stiff competition from other scavengers.

NATURE DOES IT BETTER

Even the most well-intentioned conservationists tend towards arrogance. There is an assumption that it takes human intervention to rectify the transgressions of the past. Thus a struggling population reduced by years of persecution requires human intervention to put to rectify matters with reintroductions. Or, if we need trees to improve habitats and capture the carbon pumped out by our power stations and cars, then it is man that must plant them.

In reality this is often hubris. Nature can usually do the job just as well if not better. As Iolo Williams observed, there was no need for the expensive release of Swedish and Spanish kites in England: Welsh kites would have recolonised England without help. Other once-resident birds such as ospreys and storks have returned under their own steam to claim territories from which they were driven by our ancestors.

Nature is incredibly resilient when it comes to habitats. In the absence of man, most of Europe would be forested. Obviously routine arable farming – ploughing, cultivating and spraying – prevents this, but browsers are also important. Wild animals such as deer and hares restrict the growth of scrub by nipping off the tender growing tips of seedlings, but livestock such as sheep, cattle and goats are more important in today's world.

In their absence it is incredible how quickly nature will try to revert to its pre-human state. I witnessed this when I moved here. A large area of conifers had been recently felled half a mile down the hill. It resembled the post-conflict Somme, just a mass of tumbled mud and brash. The foresters had left a few straggly rowans, birch and ash that had somehow managed to survive among the pines, but it was otherwise apparently lifeless. A new age traveller called Dave had bought the place and was constructing a shed there, much to the fury of the local planners. He claimed he wanted to make a living from the area, but in their attempts to evict him the planners insisted he must replant the trees because the felling licence stipulated the owner must replace the fallen timber. Dave's response was that as an environmentalist, he wanted to rely on natural regeneration. The planners said this was would never work, but he persisted and in the end the authorities decided that because he was clearly a loner with no interest in exploiting the planning system for profit, it was simpler to leave him alone. So he slowly added to his wooden shack, harvesting rainwater from the roof and growing a few vegetables in greenhouses made from materials salvaged from skips and tips.

Dave is long departed, leaving his shed to slowly crumble into the land, but his faith in regeneration has borne fruit. First to arrive were hundreds of birch and sallow seedlings, blown in as downy seeds. Winged ash keys arrived the same way and soon elder and holly were there too – brought in by roosting pigeons and deposited in a rich packet of fertiliser beneath their roost.

This fast-growing scrub formed the early colonisers, but the long-term victor is already beginning to appear. Oak is naturally the dominant local tree species and despite a slow start compared with the willow, ash and rowan, it is already starting to assert itself. How did these oaks arrive?

The colourful answer is on display every autumn as orange pink crows emerge from the trees.

Jays normally lurk invisibly in dense woodland, rarely seen and only betraying their presence with cackling warning calls. Indeed these are nature's trackers, with keener eyes than any Kikuyu game warden. As soon as they spot an owl, fox, stoat or polecat, off goes the harsh alarm call (as reflected in its scientific name, *Garrulus glandarius* or 'acorn chatterer'). They follow the omnivorous eating habits of other corvids, gobbling down insects, fruit, carrion, eggs and nestlings, but in autumn they leave the security of the woody glades to search for acorns beneath veteran oaks or to forage in a nearby wood. Thus for a couple of months they traverse pastures with their bouncing flight, their wings flashing white, black and electric blue.

The birds are one of the wonders of Welsh wildlife. They have incredible memories. Throughout the autumn each collects prodigious quantities of acorns – up to three thousand a month through September, October and well into November. Unlike other hoarders such as squirrels and voles that stuff hidey-holes with large stashes of seeds and nuts, jays hide each acorn individually, pushing it carefully into leaf mould or muddy ground. I have watched them flying from acorn-laden oaks into open fields to hide their prizes well away from raiding squirrels. Incredibly, in studies they were found to be able to remember the site of each nut and throughout the winter will sneak back to retrieve every one. This is where they have their secondary roles as eco-warriors, for venturing into the open to hide their treasure is risky and some inevitably fall prey to goshawks or stoats, leaving the buried acorns to germinate the following spring.

In areas grazed by livestock the saplings don't last long, but in woods or places which stock can't reach the natural dominance of the oaks takes over. They may grow at a slower pace than willow or birch, but their progress is steady and ultimately they will be taller and spread out a dense canopy which will smother the early sprinters. They are also long-lived and so over time they will elbow almost every other tree out of the way to create the woodland which once dominated most of lowland Britain.

The rapid recovery of the clear-felled bomb-site at the bottom of the valley inspired me and after ten years or so I was sufficiently excited to launch my own experiment. When we'd bought the house there was a half-acre softwood plantation behind it: a scrappy patch of neglected conifers, planted as a shelter belt in about 1960. The spindly trees had never been thinned, so were tall and lacking root-structure. This made them increasingly vulnerable to the wind – and in such conditions, as soon as one tree toppled, so it could take down its neighbour. In a bad storm, the whole plantation could be devastated overnight. I turned to Coed Cymru (Welsh Wood) for help and was sent a consultant. Andy took one look at the rangy trunks and cone-festooned tops: 'You see those pine cones?' He said. 'That's a good indicator that the trees are stressed. They sense their own mortality and are responding by trying to reproduce to keep their genes going. You need to get them down before the wind does the job for you.'

Andy helped by organising the necessary paperwork. It turns out felling is more bureaucratic than one might think. You need a licence to cut down more than five cubic metres of timber. That's roughly half a dozen decent-sized trees and although this will almost certainly be granted, one of the conditions will be that the area must be replanted at a prescribed density, although fortunately there is a modest replanting grant.

I have a chainsaw and have cut down one or two diseased trees in my time, but this was felling job was far too big a job for me to tackle. So I called in a forestry contractor to topple the trees. He was a one-man band with a small tractor and timber trailer with a grab to load the trunks. He toiled for three weeks toppling the spindly trees and cutting them to the prescribed length. Then he took them to a point where a proper timber lorry could collect the poor-quality trunks which were to be turned into fencing stakes. To my horror the wood was worth less than half the cost of the felling. But this was not about money: it was for aesthetic and environmental reasons.

Next came the replanting. Although I knew the trees would eventually take over if I fenced out stock and left the ground fallow, I didn't have Dave's patience. Nevertheless, I was running low on funds, so I felt sure I could do the replanting myself. Andy agreed this was fine, provided I stuck to the required density. This meant I needed to plant twelve hundred saplings and he pointed to the seventeen acres of hillside above my neighbour which had recently been planted by contractors. The thousands of trees were each protected by plastic rabbit guards which caught the morning sun, revealing the regimented rows marching up the slope. I had no wish to repeat this in my own 'natural' woodland and said so. Andy nodded sympathetically and said there was an answer.

'You divide the area into a grid of three metre squares and plant a spiral of a couple of dozen saplings in each,' he explained. This seemed hopelessly fiddly and bureaucratic, so once he had gone I randomly scattered the area with patches of a dozen native species: oak, ash, field maple, hazel, birch, willow, holly, wild cherry, rowan and our only native conifer – Scot's pine.

Each of the thirteen hundred whips and seedlings was given a bamboo stake and rabbit guard – commercial coiled transparent plastic for most and recycled milk containers for the pines. This took three weeks to achieve, but mainly because it was back breaking and laborious work. I then retreated, only to be dismayed by seeing my precious charges swamped by rosebay willowherb, bracken, couch grass, cleavers, brambles and nettles. For a couple of years I would wade in to inspect how my charges were faring, but soon it was impenetrable and venturing in just resulted in briar-scratched and nettle-stung legs. I naturally forgot about the patch, walking past with barely a glance and telling myself the saplings would eventually triumph.

Despite this confidence, I still noticed with surprise that the healthiest, strongest, trees were not those that I had carefully planted, staked and protected, but by far the strongest and tallest trees were self-established. The damp areas at the bottom of the hill were dominated by 'sallies' – sallow willow – which arrived in downy puffs of wind-borne seeds. The east side of the patch had plentiful elder, rowan and even holly which was the legacy of the fieldfares and pigeons which used to take shelter on the leeward edge of the conifers. The evidence of this came from the white-washed needle-covered forest floor prior to felling. Clearly those droppings had been filled with seeds. When these germinated in the guano-fertilised soil, the wild saplings were far quicker to take off and prosper than their cultivated neighbours.

The strongest trees of all were those in the dampest western corner however: whispering alder. There were a score of these growing along a nearby drainage gully and these had thrown out a mass of roots to snake invisibly beneath the pasture. Any shoots which emerged in the field would be quickly pruned by browsing sheep and cattle, but those that rose behind the protection of the woodland's fencing were safe. They also came out of the starting blocks at speed. Within a couple of years they had outgrown me and at fifteen years are now over thirty feet.

For a decade I largely ignored the wood but the same could not be said for children. My stepsons were particularly taken by the dense cover which was so much of a deterrent for me, loving to scramble into the undergrowth to play hide and seek and to create dens.

One day while I was babysitting, Arthur insisted on taking me into the trees. A lover of nature, this bright and lively eight year-old led me into the wood. To my surprise I found it was now relatively easy to penetrate – even for a six-foot man. The trees had achieved the first part of their suffocating role by killing of the bulk of the understorey. Certainly there were still sprawling briers to trip up the unwary explorer, but these had only the last threads of life and it was relatively easy to creep and crawl beneath the lower branches.

Up till now most of the clearing work has come from the wild alders, willow, rowan and elder. It is these that have been gobbling up the life-giving sun to starve the understorey into submission. But this is temporary: they are just wheeler-dealers; opportunists that grab the place by the window. The future is already in sight. Next to them the slower growing oaks, ash and Scots pine have split their rabbit guards and have no need of the bamboo stakes that once secured them against the west winds. They may still be shorter than the scrub species, but they will inevitably shoulder these out of the way. They are arboreal snow ploughs which will use their innate might and glacial strength to prevail.

The young plantation was also already producing wildlife rewards. In contrast to its dark conifer predecessor which was little more than a pigeon roost, that spring it was ringing with birdsong. As well as the resident robins, blackbirds, dunnocks and woodpeckers, there were migrant warblers, flycatchers and redstarts. When I set camera traps and put out baiting stations, I find it is regularly visited by foxes, badgers, hedgehogs and pheasants.

AUTUMN BOUNTY

One early discovery in our first year was the appearance of parasol mushrooms on the lawn. These large grassland mushrooms, which live up to their name in their appearance, have the twin benefits of being both utterly unmistakable and delicious. As a boy I had drooled over Richard Mabey's *Food for Free*, so I was fairly confident I had correctly identified them as soon as I saw them in the grass. Naturally I checked and counter-checked with various field guides and encyclopaedias and eventually plucked up the courage to try a sliver fried in butter. It was delicious! Far better than any shop mushroom I'd ever eaten.

Encouraged by this, I started to inspect local woods and quickly found members of another easily-identified family: boletes. These chunky mushrooms have sponge instead of gills and provided they are drably coloured, there are no poisonous look-alikes. At first I found only brown birch boletes which are perfectly edible, but insipid. It took a month to stumble across my first cepe. Known to Italians as porcini, this was a gastronomic revelation and thus began a growing obsession with mushroom foraging.

I went on to find chanterelles, that winter there were wood blewits and the next spring came St George's and chicken of the woods and I threw myself with increasing passion into hunts through every wood I could find. A couple of years later when some hotel-owning friends asked me to boost their season by laying on foraging breaks, the passion became professional. For the past twenty years I have been leading guided trips into the Elan Valley and nearby woods, showing the curious at least some of the huge range of delicious wild fungi that are there for the taking.

It surprises many people to discover that Wales has the perfect conditions for many of the world's most prized fungi. The climate is mild and damp – which is much better for many mushrooms than the hot dry conditions found in Italy or the Dordogne. A few years back I heard the Michelin-starred Danish chef, René Redzepi, being interviewed by Kirsty Young on *Desert Island Discs*. His Copenhagen restaurant, Noma, is ranked number one in the world, and the chef proudly boasted that he had dropped caviar from his menu in favour of chicken of the woods, a yellow bracket fungus which grows in summer on deciduous trees such as willow and oak. He described it as a fantastic but extremely rare ingredient which grows in only two places in Denmark and only three people know where these are.

This is probably hype, designed to promote the restaurant's menu, but even if it is rare in Denmark, it certainly isn't in Wales. I know of a dozen sites and when it does occur, the outcrops can be significant, weighing several kilos. I have no problems with his claims for its gastronomic excellence, for although to my mind it is nothing like chicken, it has a delicate flavour and a fantastically firm texture which makes it an infinitely superior tofu.

One potentially surprising aspect of this however is the almost total dearth of fungal knowledge in the locality. There are many good amateur naturalists locally, people who know a linnet from a twite and a willow warbler from a whitethroat. Most people also prize the myriad of whimberries that fruit in mid-summer, but virtually no one knows anything more about wild fungi than nostalgic memories of gathering field mushrooms as a child: 'I remember picking them with my grandfather,' they'll sigh. 'We'd eat them with bacon around the kitchen table for breakfast – delicious!'

Another odd thing about the best mushrooms is where they are found. Most guidebooks recommend scouring deciduous woods for choice species such as porcini, bay boletes, chanterelles and wood hedgehogs and there is certainly no shortage of oak, birch and hazel coppice. Yet after years of hunting, I find the most fruitful woods are actually mature conifer plantations. These are generally derided by conservationists as ecological deserts, artificial habitats that are so dark thanks to close planting of non-native trees that little of value can live there.

In fact the reverse is true when it comes to fungi and sometimes the crops can be prodigious. Early on in my mushroom gathering I entered one wood on a whim and left a few minutes later with around 30kg of porcini which were sliced and dried overnight on top of the wood burner. On another occasion I had taken my children to the Llangorse Climbing Centre. I had no desire to watch them clamber up and down plastic rocks for two hours so went to photograph a local waterfall only to stumble across a bumper crop of chanterelles – I picked 7kg in twenty minutes which were cleaned, flash-fried and frozen for the coming winter.

These are just two of the scores of edible species I began to discover in local woods. I learned piecemeal, adding to my repertoire one species at a time, but with the enthusiasm of a novice, I threw myself into the task and by the end of the first autumn could confidently identify a dozen. By the end of the second year I had found and tasted almost fifty. Certainly some were very much better than others and after two decades of collecting I ignore most, and porcini form the backbone of my harvesting.

These rounded fungi with their spongy pores and dark brown caps were apparently known as penny buns by our ancestors because they resemble a freshly-baked small loaf. I don't know anyone who calls them this, however: instead everyone uses the French cepes or Italian porcini. They are not the culinary ultimate – to my mind that accolade must go to the truffle, hedgehog, horn of plenty or winter chanterelle – but cepes have the great advantage of drying extremely well. Indeed, they are better when dried, for the flavour is transformed. They are clearly superior to a cultivated mushroom when fresh, but after drying they become positively nutty and intense. The flavours are released by steeping in boiling water to make a rich stock that is superb in risottos, casseroles or pasta sauces.

As I developed my obsessive interest with mushrooms, my enthusiasm was only enhanced by knowing their gastronomic qualities were as natural and organic as it is possible to get. These fungi cannot be cultivated, although man has tried hard enough over the centuries. Indeed this situation has been recognised in law. During the nineteenth century there were two prosecutions for harvesting mushrooms for sale on private property without per-mission. In both cases the judges ruled that because the landowner had done nothing to cultivate or even encourage the mushrooms – no planting, watering or weeding – they could not constitute property. In other words, they were 'an act of God' and therefore could not have been stolen.

There are a handful of mushrooms that can be grown of course, but fewer than most people realise. The familiar buttons, whites, chestnuts, flats and Portobellos are all the same species: *Agaricus bisporus*. More recently they have been joined on the supermarket shelves by shitake, oysters and even enoki, but the vast majority of the world's edible fungi simply have to be gathered from fields and forests. This means that along with some sea fish, they are about the only wild ingredients to be found in a modern supermarket where they command high prices on the 'world cooking' aisles. This made my genuine Welsh porcini taste all the better and reinforced my sense of *cynefin* as I stared at the rows of clip-topped Kilner jars in the store cupboard. Better still was the sense of warmth and belonging when I could cook a huge winter casserole of home-reared duck legs, flavoured with root vegetables and the earthy tones of porcini stock.

The discovery that conifer plantations could be rich hunting grounds was a powerful incentive to wander further afield than I would normally. In the evenings I would scan maps for the biggest woods I could find. Several of these were to the north east of Rhayader, towards Bwlch y Sarnau and above the tiny village of Abbey Cwmhir. The latter is named after the huge gothic monastery whose ruins are still visible in its heart. Despite the remote setting, the abbey was conceived on a vast scale during the twelfth century. Its backers were the Mortimers, the great Marcher lords that were briefly the most powerful aristocrats in England. When the plans were originally drawn up it was to be one of the largest buildings in Europe, with a nave longer than either Canterbury or Salisbury Cathedrals.

The abbey was never completed because the Mortimers' fortunes tumbled after Roger, First Earl of March, fell from royal favour. He had rebelled against Edward II, taking the king's wife, Isabella as his mistress and deposing the monarch. He probably also arranged his murder in 1327, seized lands from other great magnates and was de facto ruler for the next three years as regent for the young Edward III. Not surprisingly, this made him powerful enemies and in 1330, as his ward reached maturity, he rounded on his guardian to accuse him of treason and Roger was summarily hanged at Tyburn.

Today the Abbey is little more than a few tumbled walls, but is significant for nationalists as the last resting place of the decapitated

Llywelyn ap Gruffudd, last of the Welsh princes. Having led initially successful acts of defiance towards Edward I, he suffered a series of setbacks. Hemmed in by his enemies in Snowdonia, in 1282 he fled south to raise another rebellion, reputedly spending his last night in a small cave near Aberedw, a few miles from Builth and was killed nearby the next day. Given the fall from grace of the Mortimers some fifty years later, it seems ironic it was Roger's uncle, Roger de Chirk, who carried Llewellyn's head to London to present to Edward I.

My fungal interest in the village is also linked to history, albeit of much more recent origin. The biggest building in today's village is the Victorian 'Hall' which was built by a wealthy local family. As was the fashion, they established an arboretum. A century later the Forestry Commission bought much of the neglected estate and planted it with the ubiquitous sitkas that cover the Welsh uplands. However, the new owners left the existing exotics such as beech and maples and as the conifers have matured, this has created a rich mosaic of fungal habitats. Thus porcini, bay boletes and deceivers thrive in symbiotic relationships with the pines, while chanterelles, winter chanterelles and wood hedgehogs love the beeches. And the plentiful fallen timber and rotting stumps from thinning operations are perfect for honey fungus.

THE HUNTING DRIVE

The obsessive scouring of new woodlands has other benefits. I've already mentioned that I think any sort of hunting opens one's eyes to the world around. The search for good mushroom patches also drives one to explore remote areas as one mines for richer fungal seams. One particularly magical experience came when I visited a distant plantation two or three miles from the nearest house. It was on a hilltop and as I approached it a huge vista opened up to the west with views stretching twenty miles to the Cambrian watershed beyond the Elan Valley. My eye was caught by movement above the pasture next to the road and I watched entranced as a tiny hawk sped past – a small blue-backed bird which resembled a peregrine, but it was far too small and its head was tinted russet. It was a merlin, or to be precise for its russet-tinted head showed it to be an adult male, or jack. This is Britain's smallest raptor, squeezing in a whisker below a male sparrowhawk, or musket, and he was clearly searching for pipits. He was presumably hoping either to surprise one of these ubiquitous small brown birds out in the open or, better still, happen across one in flight.

Merlins used to be known as the lady's hawk and were traditionally flown at skylarks in what is one potentially one of the most spectacular sights in falconry. The songbird has a much lower wing loading than the little falcon and tries to escape by flying up almost vertically, singing as it climbs. The merlin is faster but has to gain altitude by flying in tight circles. It is an entirely natural hunt, one which occurs unseen above Britain's moors and downs every day, and both birds know that victory goes to the highest. In a good flight, the pair will go up and up until they are out of sight and the only indication the hunt is still going is the lark's beautiful bubbling song. Usually the chorister stays above the falcon and escapes, but if its pursuer can get above it the tables are turned and the faster hawk will have the upper hand. This is when the lark bales out and plummets to earth, pursued by a predator that is only a fraction bigger than its quarry. I kept watching this little hunter, hoping he would get lucky, but it was not to be and in no time he was flitting off down the valley to vanish against the backdrop of the browns and greens of a Welsh late summer.

My serious mushroom hunting takes place in September and October. This starts with my own private hunts and then becomes the more organised forays for paying guests. These are time and energy consuming, so I only start the process of reclaiming the goshawk in mid-October. Much as I may be addicted to falconry, it is as seasonal as almost everything in the countryside. One can only really fly a goshawk while the leaves are off the trees – otherwise she almost instantly disappears and even if this doesn't lead to her loss (her bells and telemetry should still reveal her location), it can be extremely stressful. More importantly it negates the whole point of the sport which is to watch a supreme hunter in action. In fact I often think of it as bird watching for the lazy. Despite living in an area which is heaving with raptors and owls, in a quarter of a century I have only seen a handful of genuine pursuits and the barn owl catching a vole soon after our arrival is almost the only kill.

So, I fly Sky from about September to February and she spends the summer moulting. As a result as soon as the leaves start to show signs of turning I begin the process of training her up again – or reclaiming as falconers know the process – and this ties in neatly with my fungi forays. The main mushroom season dwindles to a halt as the last leaves fall from the trees, leaving me free to concentrate on the hawk. For the next three or four months I can fly her in local fields and woods, catching squirrels, rabbits and the occasional pheasant. Not that she catches very much, for there never seems to be very much around. When she does see something, however, she really demonstrates why goshawks have been so revered by falconers for at least two, and possibly as many as fifteen, millennia. This really is an apex predator, explosive in her acceleration and frightening in her power.

I am actually not interested in killing except that this is the integral motivation for the hawk. Sky is descended from countless generations of killers and the sight of fleeing feather or fur triggers instincts she cannot control. In an explosive start from the fist that would put Usain Bolt to shame, she powers off after the quarry and, far more often than not, has it tightly gripped in her feet within seconds. And the power in those feet is awesome. When really pumped up – typically after just missing a squirrel or rabbit – she would land on my glove, gripping tightly and massaging my thumb and finger through the three layers of thick buckskin.

She exerts massive pressure through those feet and is almost incapable of letting go as I try to weigh her. Now for most of the year I would happily have her on my bare hand – normally I trust her completely – but when she's really fired up, every time she detects the slightest movement between her claws she wriggles them back and forth, exerting a pulsating vice-like grip. Were my hand to be unguarded, they would easily go straight through the palm. When really pumped up she refuses to let go of the glove even after I have put her on the perch and I have to slip my hand out, leaving it with her to retrieve later.

One of my chief motivations for keeping and flying hawks is

that it motivates me in much the same way that walking the dog encourages millions of other Britons to take exercise. One morning, as I tethered Sky on her bow perch on the lawn, I heard sounds from Bwlch y Llys, the house further up the hill. I knew it had changed hands recently, for the previous owners had sent me an e-mail announcing their departure and wishing me well. This house has changed hands four times since I got here.

Nestling in the sheltered side of the mountain behind our house, it is a Victorian building, but it is built on the ruins of others. Clearly the site is good – all old homesteads around here have a good water supply and are sheltered from the worst of the elements – but in the modern world some seem mildly 'cursed'. By that I mean the owners seem to sell up with remarkable regularity. All around Wales there seems to be a selection of apparently lovely houses that appear to be perpetually on the market. Or rather estate agents boards go up and down every couple of years or so. This pattern often persists for decades. Some must have been sold and resold nearly a dozen times over the past quarter century: clearly there is something wrong with life there, some hidden problem, which reasserts itself with each new owner. Perhaps it's a difficult neighbour, or maybe the house is in a frost pocket or services such as television, broadband and telephone are lacking? Whatever the case, the same suspects keep being flagged up for sale.

I suspect Bwlch y Llys probably suffers from being on the east side of a steep hill. This means it suffers from a lack of light for much of the autumn, winter and spring. The owners have all been lovely people, but they haven't lasted. Some have made great improvements. The last couple stayed longer than most, planting seventeen acres of mixed broadleaf woodland above the house, converting the garage into a luxurious two-bedroomed flat and digging three huge pools which were teeming with wildlife within months. Eventually they also left, victims of aging joints, to spend their last of their retirement in the South of France.

Good neighbourly relations are important in an area such as this, so I was obviously keen to make friends with the new owners who arrived a couple of months later. I kept putting things off, however, although I heard various snippets of gossip about the newcomers. They were a couple and he was a retired military man: 'a thoroughly nice chap' I was assured by my chainsaw mechanic, but the meeting had to wait because they took their time moving down permanently from their London base. They clearly made regular preparatory visits, however, because over the summer I sporadically heard the sound of machinery. The rampant foliage between our properties meant I couldn't see what was going on, but most of the engines sounded like lawnmowers or strimmers which might well be a local gardener doing routine maintenance.

That autumn morning, as I struggled to tie the hawk's leash with half-frozen fingers, I heard the steady and unmistakable undulating whine of saws from the hill above. Later this was followed by the noise of a big chipper steadily chewing boughs all afternoon. This meant some fairly major tree surgery and the scale of work that a new owner would probably want to oversee. It was time to introduce myself and I decided the best way to make a positive impact was to arrive with a hawk. I am extremely biased here, but I find it generally creates a very strong impression to meet someone with a magnificent large female gos on their fist.

Over the following fortnight I had three thwarted attempts at engineering a meeting when the hawk appeared determined to fly down the valley rather than climb the hill. Each time I set off with her and the excited dog, climbing the steep slope behind the house, she would sheer off down the lane on the most familiar route. Call as hard as I could, she was intent on reaching the relatively rich pickings of the valley bottom. Goshawks are often branded as stupid, but in reality they are cunning and remember past kills. Sky was well aware there were likely to be far more squirrels and pheasants in the hedges and coppices than on the bracken-covered hilltop, but on the fourth attempt I had her keen enough to follow me up the mountain. This is another word which has its origins in falconry, referring to the sharpness of the breastbone of the hawk ('sharp-set' has the same roots). In the days before weighing machines, a falconer would judge the motivation of his hawk by feeling its chest. This is where any fat reserves are first built up, thus a pronounced keel (breast) bone denotes a bird with muscle, but no excess fat and sufficiently motivated to fly safely.

We headed up the steep slope behind the house, the spaniel puppy running exuberantly across the fields and through the bracken and gorse. As we reached the top of the hill, the hawk became more independent – as is her wont – and flew to a range of vantage points to survey the valley below. I let her have her head, calling her back every few minutes for a reward. She was obliging at first and we were overlooking the neighbours when things took a different turn. Normally the prevailing west wind whips along our minor valley and – thanks to the protection of the mountain – leaves most of the upper hillside behind the house in comparative shelter. This, is after all, where Bwlch y Llys ('sheltered gap') gets its name.

That day there was a stiff southerly breeze coming up the Wye Valley and instead of the hillside being in a comparative calm, this created a natural updraft. As Sky returned to my upraised hand for the fifth time, she caught the rising air in her sails to give her a natural lift. She was suddenly like a child riding on an escalator for the first time. She couldn't resist the unexpected free lift. Normally she flies hard and fast on pumping wings, but now her wings suddenly set rigidly as she let the air currents do the work. She was soaring like a buzzard, although her wings are considerably more pointed and she looked surprisingly falcon-like as she glided in wide circles above the slope, climbing with each circuit and ranging ever-wider over the valley.

It was November but it was a late year and autumn was still in full flow. It really was stunning! Surely no painter could have mixed a richer palette of yellows, golds, ochres, russets, browns and blacks against the rich green pastures of a warm autumn? This was a natural version of Gustav Klimt's 'The Kiss': a natural version of his painting of two lovers locked in an embrace beneath a garish patchwork quilt. And while I looked at the explosion of vibrant colours that ironically represent the seasonal death of plant life, so I felt it seemed a celebration of life as well.

When flying, no falconer can think of anything other than his hawk for more than a few seconds and no sooner had I appreciated the colours and scenery than I was focussed on the bird. She really was stunning – flying in a manner far more reminiscent of a peregrine than her normal goshawk hunting mode. Rather than flying hard, low and fast above the ground, she was soaring like the ever-present buzzards, circling on the invisible lift of the updrafts and the thermals rising from the valley bottom. This gave her all the speed and lift she required.

As if to display the contrasting ways of flying effortlessly, a dozen kites and ravens soared a few hundred feet above, their wings also rigid, but they were circling far more slowly. It was clear from their movements and calls that they could see her. They didn't like her presence at all, knowing that if she was presented with an opportunity she would be only too ready to attack, but they also knew that as long as they kept above her, they were safe. She was too intent her effortless flight to bother to chase them and instead continued to range over the valley, now interspersing her long glides with rapid wing beats as she circled ever wider. I stood entranced, but not entirely comfortable. On the one hand it was wonderful to see her revelling in her total freedom, rolling on the air currents and clearly knowing she was mistress of her domain, but on the other hand the same realisation was simultaneously disquieting. I could try to call her back at any time by offering a tempting morsel of meat on my outstretched glove, but she was so lost in the joys of flight I wasn't sure how much appeal this would have. If she chose to ignore me there was nothing I could do.

I watched her heart in mouth for what felt like an age, but was almost certainly no more than a minute or two. Suddenly I could bear it no more and I pulled out the lure which hawks generally find more attractive than food on the fist. Traditionally this is supposed to represent the quarry you want your hawk to hunt and is garnished with a large lump of meat. Thus buzzards might be called to a fur covered pad dragged along the ground which is supposed to resemble a rabbit while a bird hunter such as a peregrine would be lured back with a pair of dried wings whirled above the falconer's head.

I am not a traditionalist when it comes to lures. Some years ago I read *Understanding the Bird of Prey* by the Carmarthenshire-based Nick Fox. He points out that a hawk is an instinctive hunter with such fantastic eyesight that it is never going to be fooled into thinking a pair of wings is a bird or some faux fur sausage is a rabbit. Moreover such lures are impossible to sterilise and are breeding grounds for bacteria.

Instead Fox suggests shredded car inner tube tied with a swivel to a braided cotton cord. The hawk is trained to associate this with a really big food reward in the relatively early stages of training. In my case I used an entire dead quail which I threw in front of her while she was still tethered to her perch on the lawn. This little game bird has rich flesh hidden beneath its feathers and among its bones. As a result she spent a happy afternoon plucking and dismantling the corpse and all the while building a powerful mental link between an enjoyable feast and the black rubber. She was flying free the next time I brought out the lure and she came in instantly to crash into the black rubber with its quail garnish and to stand there defiantly on top of her prize, beak slightly agape. I approached slowly and cautiously to defuse any suspicion she might have that I was trying to steal her meal and carefully tethered her to the ground where she stood. I then left her to gorge again. This is another word originating from falconry, because the hawk's crop is in its throat (*la gorge* in French) and this is swollen after a good meal. After these two recalls she was as hooked as any crack addict.

After this the garnish was no longer necessary. While hawks are much more intelligent than most animal behaviourists give them credit, they are also driven largely by instinct and once the bird is *wedded* to the fluttering black rubber, she will come in just for the joy of catching this easy 'kill'. Merely the sight of the flapping black rubber is the proverbial red rag to a bull and she finds it irresistible, hurtling in to foot the rubber and to be rewarded with a lump of meat on the fist while I slip the lure into my hawking vest pocket. This has become my failsafe method of recapture.

Abandoning the meat on the lure is a good idea because not only does this reduce bacteria, but also because it is easy for the meat to become detached. The last thing and falconer wants is a hawk which is already reluctant to return to fly off with a large lump of meat. Also, it is horribly easy to forget that there is a garnished lure in the hawking vest. In warm weather this has particularly unpleasant results when a questing hand detects movement and finds the pocket is full of wriggling maggots. This is deeply nauseating, but every falconer has done it.

On this occasion I pulled out the lure and swung it around my head. At first the distant brown hawk appeared to pay no attention and instead carried on her wide circles above the valley. It was a heart-stopping moment. If she were to go into a complete reverie and fly further and further afield, at best I would have a long, frustrating, search around the valley, waving the unwieldy antennae to pick up the signal from her tail-mounted radio transmitter. At worst it could mean her total loss. To my relief, however, after half a minute or so she wheeled around and seemed to head in my direction.

I lost sight of her against the background of wooded hills, but the distant tinkling of bells became louder. I let out an audible breath of relief and relaxed. A moment later she was at my feet, stamping and striking at the shredded rubber, while mantling over her inert prey. I brandished a chicken wing in front of her and a few moments later she'd abandoned the rubber for my fist to tear meat and sinew from the bones. This is what falconers know as a tiring – a piece of meat that looks bigger than it really is, but it takes time and work to rip apart, building up her shoulder muscles and giving me time to fit her jesses, swivel and leash. As a safety precaution I tied her with a falconer's knot to the metal ring on the glove. I then walked down the hill, crossing a couple of fences to approach the bottom fence of the neighbour's property. I was met with a smile and the two dogs sniffed each other and started to play. Both were about nine months old, apparently. Lydia was remarkably unphased by the hawk, but friendly. She and her husband Richard had now eased themselves out of London life and were moving in for good. They had already fallen in love with the area and its wildlife.

As I retreated to my own domain I couldn't help feeling that the afternoon demonstrates how the simplest of walks is immeasurably enhanced by the hawk and dog. I can vicariously harness the animals' senses. The hawk's eyesight and the dog's sense of smell are both infinitely better than my own, so by watching their behaviour in the field I see far more than I could ever hope to detect on my own. This is hunting, but more in the sense of questing than a chase culminating in a kill. Merely the intention of 'capturing' something on a walk opens one's eyes to a host of other observations.

So while flying Sky I am tuned in to everything in the hedge bottoms. Yes, I might be looking for signs of movement denoting a pheasant or squirrel, but while peering into the undergrowth I spot wood blewits, clouded funnels, knight's shield and poison pie mushrooms. There is a last blackberry clinging to a bramble and a little further on the holly berries are starting to deepen from dark orange to deep Christmas crimson. And I'd never noticed how much ivy there is curling around the roots of the blackthorn and hazel hedgerows – coating the ground and an invaluable source of autumn pollen for my bees which are starting to head towards winter dormancy.

This heightened appreciation of nature underlies the popularity of fishing locally. It feels as if every local man is a member of the Rhayader Angling Association. Fishing is often cited as Britain's most popular participant sports with millions of men (and they are overwhelmingly men) spending countless hours trying to coax wild fish onto hooks. In most of Britain this means coarse fishing where the angler dangles baited hooks into slow-moving or still water. Here it almost exclusively fly fishing – the art of fooling a trout, grayling or salmon into mouthing a hook hidden beneath feather, fur and tinsel.

Fly fishing has traditionally been a rich man's pastime. Indeed, locally it is at the root of serious social unrest. The Rebecca Riots, where toll gates were uprooted by men dressed as women with blacked-up faces, lasted only a few months, but the rebelliousness lived on. The target of their resentment and social and political defiance switched to the rivers. The English aristocracy had just discovered the delights of fly fishing for salmon and began to flock to the great rivers of Wales and Scotland, building lodges and houses along the banks. In much the same way that most of Britain's commons were privatised through the Inclosure Acts of the eighteenth and nineteenth centuries, fishing rights were first created and then bought and sold for huge sums completely out of reach of any farmer, let alone labourer. The migratory fish had been a staple of local diets for centuries, but suddenly locals were told the right to take them from the Wye and its tributaries now belonged to rich Englishmen, and bailiffs patrolled the banks. Woe betide the local man caught with a fish.

The traditional fishing method was far more productive than flicking a feather-adorned hook across the waters. The salmon and brown trout which drew the wealthy anglers to the Wye and its tributaries spawn in autumn. They move up the Bristol Channel and into freshwater in spring and spend the summer in the deeper, slower moving waters, barely feeding, while waiting for the first serious rains of late autumn. These raise water levels and when the river is in spate, the big salmon are able to move up the smaller tributaries to get to the normally inaccessible gravel banks in the shallows.

Just as predictable as the move by the spawning salmon was the rush by the men of Rhayader and the surrounding farms to their attics, sheds and barns. There they would uncover the gaffs which had lain hidden and unused for the past eleven months. A gaff is a specialised harpoon. There are various designs, but the commonest comes in the form of a huge barbed hook which is lashed tightly to a stick. The poacher wades out onto the spawning grounds, armed with a torch and strikes at the mating fish. If successful, he would haul the catch onto the bank. In the glory days of the late nineteenth and early twentieth centuries, when the Wye was the premier salmon fishery in Britain, many if not most of the local men would be on the spawning beds on dark nights, harvesting the wild bounty in scenes which would have been akin to the human equivalent of Alaskan grizzlies and bald eagles feasting on sockeye salmon.

The catch would be sold in the relatively affluent Midlands, picked up by colluding train guards who would take boxes of fish from the poachers as the trains slowed to a crawl on the uphill stretches of line (it was convenient for the poachers that one of the slowest stretches of track was just above the most productive spawning bed). There was good money to be made from salmon, particularly during the years of rationing during and just after the war.

Harvesting spawning trout was less lucrative, but also made a significant contribution to local diets and income. These smaller fish were generally not gaffed, but speared with long-handled barbed forks made specially by the local blacksmith, and catching them was considerably less risky than fishing for salmon, because trout breed further upstream in some of the smallest brooks rather than the well-known gravel banks which are generally within a few hundred yards of the Wye itself.

Like the gaff hooks they would be hidden away from prying eyes in nooks and crannies for the authorities did everything they could to stamp out poaching. Water bailiffs and the police would patrol the riverbanks, looking for the tell-tale flash of a shrouded storm lantern which would reveal the presence of a gang at work. When poachers were caught they were locked up overnight and dragged in front of the magistrates at the earliest opportunity. Indeed, in autumn poaching hearings were one of the most frequent autumn offences at the magistrates hearings in Rhayader and Llanidloes.

There was more to poaching than money-making. The fish might sell well, but there was also a strong element of class friction at work. Locals resented the way that a traditional natural harvest had been sequestrated, thus taking salmon from under the very noses of the rich incomers who had appropriated their natural heritage was cocking a snook at authority. The classic poacher's defence that a wild animal cannot belong to anyone until it has been caught certainly held true. This is evident from the way in which the poachers would not only black their faces for their nocturnal fishing trips – an eminently sensible bit of camouflage when trying to dodge the bailiffs and police – but until well into the twentieth century many would don the traditional skirts and shawls of their wives and mothers, harking back to the days of Rebecca. To this day local pubs are decorated with faded photographs of grinning men, faces blackened with soot and tallow, dressed in skirts and dark jackets, surrounded by salmon.

The glory days of poaching are long-gone, mainly because the fishery collapsed during the 1980s, but also because fish farming saw the price of fish tumble. At the same time the authorities, deeply alarmed at tumbling stocks drastically increased the penalties. Now it was no longer a £20 or £30 fine which could easily be covered by the income from another night's poaching, but instead anyone caught in the act faced the confiscation of all equipment – which included the vehicles which were essential to reach the least conspicuous spawning beds and fines could reach four figures.

Thus widespread poaching became a thing of the past, yet

despite this some persists – again more an act of rebellion, enhanced with a big dash of tradition. Finding those that do it takes diplomacy for the penalties remain high. Nevertheless, soon after arriving here I was commissioned by *The Guardian* to write a piece on poaching, conditional on an interview with a practicing poacher. I spent some time asking around, eventually being directed to talk to the landlord of one of Rhayader's many pubs. My clumsy enquiries were met with a stony stare: 'There's none of that goes on here now,' he said without a hint of a smile. 'I'd forget about it if I were you.'

I asked several luminaries of the local angling club and was met with the same blank wall. Eventually, just as I was about to phone my editor to admit defeat, an electrician came to fix a constantly tripping fuse. I mentioned my difficulties finding a genuine poacher and he smiled: 'I know just the man you need to talk to,' he said. 'I'm drinking with him tonight – I'll see if he's willing to talk.'

He was. The next afternoon I went over to his house where he was nursing a monumental hangover (the previous night's drinking session had finished at 4am). After an hour or two's chatting in his living room, we went down to one of the most famous spawning beds and, probably because he was still drunk, Bob (not his real name), demonstrated how to gaff a fish. He took the shepherd's crook I was using as a walking stick for a prop and after spotting two large salmon with his practiced eye, he inched towards them. The fish were each about the length of my forearm and were sheltering in a quiet hollow just below the crashing water of a set of falls.

Holding the stick by the bottom, slowly he lowered the curved and polished sheep's horn handle into the water, manoeuvring it beneath the fish. Then, with a sudden jerk, he pulled up. The fish was propelled momentarily out of the water, but instead of landing on the bank as Bob had intended, the thrashing fish rose clear of the water in a momentary silver flash above the torrent. Then there was a huge splash as the cock (Bob always claimed to take only cocks in order to preserve stocks) fell back into the foaming peat-yellowed water.

Having cracked the local omerta, I slowly discovered Bob was far from unique. While the vast majority of anglers and farmers are entirely law-abiding, there is hard core of traditionalists that go out to 'take a fish' each autumn. For some this is almost a superstition. On one occasion, following a rather boozy evening in a pub, three local luminaries offered to take me out looking for trout high in the Cambrians. We went out, memorably, on Halloween along the highest of the Elan Valley's reservoirs, leaving the tarred road to drive for two or three miles along a track leading to a long-deserted farmhouse. The night was as dark as one might possibly imagine, clouds obscuring the moon and stars. The chances of being apprehended in such a remote location were vanishingly small, yet still we shrouded our torches and spoke in whispers as if convinced that bailiffs and police would rise out of the surrounding tussocks of molinia or moor grass.

The expedition had been prompted by beer-fuelled bravado and was fruitless, but slowly over the years I have discovered low-level poaching is actually fairly widespread, albeit at an ecologically inconsequential level. From my bedroom window, for example, I can see a farm whose owner – a dyed in the wool traditionalist – insists on eating a salmon poached from the brook beneath his home for Christmas dinner each year. He is definitely old-school, a mischievous man in his seventies who takes one or two fish a year from the stream because 'it's my brook and I'm not having any suits-worth telling me what I can do with my water'.

On another occasion a young hedger, still in his twenties, asked me to identify some wild mushrooms he'd found whilst laying an overgrown nearby boundary. We went through his Tupperware container which was crammed with late autumn species – wood blewits, honey fungus, shaggy ink caps and the inevitable clouded agaric. He half-knew what he was doing, so had picked carefully and as a result all four were edible to some degree. He ended our brief session in my kitchen with: 'You like fish don't you?' I was slightly puzzled, but nodded. Two weeks later, a few days before Christmas, I returned home with the children after school to find a two-kilo salmon with a tell-tale gash in its side on the doorstep. There was no note, but there was one very small wild mushroom, a Jew's ear, the tawny-brown pink gelatinous fungus that grows on elder around the year, perched on its side above the wound.

The fish was big, but just small enough to fit in my stovetop hot smoker. I'd cut down a wild plum while trimming a hedge a few months before and had put the logs to one side to use for sawdust rather than fuel. Judicious use of the saw meant that by cutting along the grain rather than across, I ended up with a huge pile of frothy shavings. These went into the base of the smoker and the gutted salmon, having been marinated overnight with a rub of salt and sugar, was then lightly cooked in the sweet smoke from the shavings. It tasted sublime, needless to say, the taste only enhanced by its illicit wild origins and the knowledge that the shavings came from a tree I had personally planted.

I have no personal problems with the concept of a local person taking the occasional fish, however depleted the general river stocks might be. Poaching is not responsible for the catastrophic decline in salmon numbers in the Wye. Locals have always taken salmon for food and in the past catches were far higher, yet the fish were always there. Clearly the problems are down to novel factors. It seems most probable that large-scale catches at sea and changes in river management are the principle reasons for the collapse in stocks and poaching is just a convenient scapegoat. On the plus side, however, salmon are incredibly prolific and if conditions are right they could easily mount a spectacular come back.

Also all the neighbours who have sheepishly admitted to taking the occasional fish share Bob's claim that they only target cocks on the basis that fates of future generations rest mainly with the hens. One cock can 'cover' a dozen females, moving around the bed, swimming alongside a bedding female and releasing his milt in a milky cloud as she begins to shed her orange eggs into the hollow in the gravel. Bob was certainly convinced that his activities made absolutely no difference.

CYNEFIN

I was told recently that the great landscape historian, Oliver Rackham, believed Britain's native hazels may be doomed to a lingering extinction because marauding grey squirrels are so efficient at harvesting unripe cobs that they never get a chance to fall to ground and germinate. I suspect this is yet another scare story, an example of the ecological xenophobia with which we view almost all non-native species. There is a very good exposition of this argument in *The New Wild* by Fred Pearce. He spins a complex web of arguments about the impact of introduced species on ecosystems around the world, but the basic tenet is that the overwhelming tide of conventional environmental thought – that 'aliens' are almost always detrimental – is seriously over-stated.

Pearce argues non-native species rarely succeed in colonising new territories in practice, not least because by definition they have not evolved over hundreds of thousands of years to thrive in their new surroundings. As a result he estimates some ninety-nine per cent of deliberate or accidental introductions fail. When they do succeed, this is generally because there is a vacant ecological niche which usually means the impact on other native plants and fauna is relatively minimal. Even when there are negative consequences, these tend to be over-stressed by conservationists and in most cases a natural equilibrium is established within a few years.

Wales certainly has its fair share of successful non-native species, but then in many ways this is because it has more than its share of vacant niches. As the glaciers retreated at the end of the last Ice Age, there was a relatively narrow time window for mammals, reptiles and amphibians to wander, slither or hop into southern England before the Dogger and Atlantic seas connected to create the barrier of the Channel. Some aliens, such as brown hares, fallow deer and rabbits were introduced a couple of millennia ago, but more recently we have acquired Canada geese, Japanese knotweed, muntjac, wild boar and signal crayfish. All of these have been castigated as unwanted 'plagues' at some point in their history, but actually even those that apparently create the worst problems also bring less-heralded benefits. Rabbits, for example, were originally a valuable source of human food for first the aristocracy and clergy, but later they became regarded more as a troublesome agricultural pest, although they remained a dietary mainstay for the urban poor.

Meanwhile they had become an important part of wild ecosystems. Buzzards, stoats and polecats all became specialist rabbit hunters, while opportunistic predators such as foxes, eagles and goshawks also cashed in. The most unusual example of a rabbit-dependent species is the large blue butterfly. Its reproductive cycle relies on an ant which takes the butterfly's larvae back to their nest as food. This is thwarted by the caterpillars which exude a pheromone which stops the ants from eating them and instead the butterflies overwinter underground in the safety of the ant colony to emerge the next spring as a flying adult. The problem was that the ants are very heat-sensitive and their colonies are on south-facing slopes covered with short, rabbit-cropped, grass. When myxomatosis decimated the rabbits on the southern chalk downs, the ants and butterflies disappeared as well.

More recently, the much loathed signal crayfish might have carried a fungal disease which threatens their native white-clawed relatives, but their numbers have exploded in British waterways just as eel populations have crashed. The latter were the mainstay of otter diets until recently, but signals are now a plentiful source of protein to take their place. Japanese knotweed is in a similar category. It was accidentally introduced around fifty years ago as an escapee from horticultural collections and soon became plant public enemy number one, so loathed that its presence on a property spells rejection of any mortgage application. Its UK stronghold is Swansea which was heavily bombed during the Second World War and then suffered from a lack of investment for many years. As a result large areas of waste ground were left to their own devices for many years – the perfect conditions for this plant. After some years the Council realised there was a problem with this hardy perennial and it appointed a knotweed officer who soon became Britain's acknowledged expert on the plant. He proselytised on its evils, produced estimates of the millions of pounds of economic damage it caused every year and advised that it was so strong-growing it could destroy buildings by coming up through concrete and foundations. Most of these reports appear exaggerated (he did have to justify his job after all), but in an interesting development trials suggest an Asian bug could be a form of natural control. Many past attempts at introducing a second alien species to control an invasive problem have not been successful (for example importing foxes to control rabbits and cane toads to eat cane beetles to Australia were disastrous). In this case, however, there is a primitive psyllid (a plant louse related to aphids) which lives solely on knotweed sap, so in theory should have no impact on any native plants. Meanwhile, it's worth noting that in its home nation knotweed is valued as a food and that various semi-professional British foragers are starting to harness its edible qualities in pickles and liqueurs.

To return to Pearce's central argument, however, he points out that until about 1950 our ancestors were positively in favour of introductions. The Victorians were generally optimists. They were surrounded by examples of how man could improve the natural world – be it by pumping water from aquifers to make deserts bloom, crossing Italian and native honey bees or adding a dash of colour to Britain's lakes and rivers by releasing mandarin ducks. Such introductions were 'exotics': a positive word which implies exciting and glamorous. Eminent Victorians such as the Dukes of Bedford and Frank Buckland were passionate advocates of introductions and were lauded for their efforts to enlarge the range of British fauna. Successive governments enthusiastically backed agricultural diversification by encouraging smallholders and crofters to try mink, muskrat and coypu farming. The general attitudes changed sharply with the Cold War. Almost overnight the experimental exotic creatures and plants released by the Victorians and Edwardians as quaint or useful additions to the British countryside were being labelled 'alien' and 'invasive'.

The debate is much more complex than is often presented, but in most of lowland Britain, one of the most disliked newcomers is the grey squirrel. This was accidentally released in Bedfordshire some hundred and twenty years ago and is now firmly established as one of our commonest mammals. At the same time, the native red 'Squirrel Nutkin' has all but vanished. There are strong links between the two phenomena. Greys are bigger, more aggressive, and apparently carry a parvo-virus to which they are immune, but which is fatal to the reds. As a result the greys are now found almost everywhere in England and Wales and they appear to have totally evicted the reds throughout this range. The natives are confined to Scotland and a few geographically isolated pockets such as Anglesey and the Isle of Wight.

Actually, the picture might not be as bleak as this. Well before the arrival of the greys, red squirrels were subject to 'boom and bust' population explosions, often linked to acorn and nut crops. Also, while they might now be viewed fondly, they were persecuted ruthlessly as pests until the 1930s. They also appear to be clinging on in some areas – such as small pockets of the Cambrian Mountains – where they are officially extinct. I've never seen one locally, but I know they have been caught on film by camera traps near Tregaron and a postman told me he'd seen them in the Elan Valley comparatively recently.

In addition, as smaller, lighter, creatures, red squirrels are better suited to life in the conifer forests which now dominate so much of Britain's forestry. In contrast, greys are tougher, more omnivorous – so more prone to raid songbird nests - and while they are at home in any woodland, they thrive among broadleaves. Fans of the native reds have some reasons for hope, however, for apparently they are much more capable of co-existing with pine martens. The latter may be proficient climbers, but they are far bigger than the small native squirrels which can evade them by climbing along the thinnest twigs in the upper canopy. In contrast the introduced greys have not evolved alongside martens and also spend more time on the ground where they are more vulnerable to this fast predator that is perfectly capable of pursuing them at speed up a tree trunk. This is certainly the conclusion of some Irish studies and the recent introductions of this arboreal weasel to Mid-Wales might be the vital boost that saves the vestigial population.

There are also plenty of examples of relatively recent introductions which no one would want to reverse. Mandarin ducks, for example, are such stunning birds (or at least the drakes are) that no one would like to see them removed from our inland waters. And interestingly there are now more of these Asian waterfowl in the wild in Britain than in their native China. The little owl is another nineteenth century import which has been welcomed with open arms. It was associated in Greek mythology with the goddess of wisdom (its scientific name, *Athene noctua*, means 'Athene by night') and their characteristic forms were stamped on Athenian coins. Over time they became synonymous with the city, thus accounting for the association of owls with wisdom. All of this greatly appealed to the Classics-loving Victorian gentry and one aristocrat in particular, the fourth Lord Lilford, introduced scores to his Northamptonshire estate in the 1890s. Not content with that, when visiting friends around the country, he would take pairs of these diminutive owls as gifts for his hosts.

The birds increased rapidly, spreading across England and Wales, largely because they flew into a vacant ecological niche. Although they follow the general owl liking for small mammals, most of their calories come from insects and worms. Better still, being nocturnal they face virtually no competition for food from other birds, so their main rivals are hedgehogs and badgers.

As natives of the Mediterranean, British conditions are at the limit of their range and they are certainly absent from the Welsh Uplands, but I have seen them on Skomer, sitting glumly on drystone walls blinking as they are dive-bombed by outraged swallows. Incidentally this is also the only place I have seen short-eared owls which are at home in the tree-less conditions, for they are ground-nesters and like to hunt in open country. Their presence on Skomer and Skokholm is a mixed blessing for bird lovers because these islands are free of ground predators such as stoats, foxes and rats, making them ideal breeding grounds for shearwaters and petrels. These spend nine months of the year hunting way out at sea and as a result are clumsy and naïve on land, making them easy targets for great black backed gulls and ravens. Their solution is to spend the hours of daylight fishing way out at sea and only returning after dark to feed their solitary youngster. This has worked well until comparatively recently when the short-eared owls arrived on the islands and they are wreaking a terrible toll among the sea birds. The problem poses particular problems for bird lovers. Elsewhere organisations such as the RSPB quietly control ground predators like foxes and rats on reserves with a lot of ground-nesting birds, but these are plentiful and, let's face it, mammals. The charity has a major problem when the threats are other birds. Many studies show raptors pose major issues on grouse moors, for example, while magpies, crows, skuas, gulls and owls can be issues in other areas.

CONCLUSION

Much has changed over the quarter of a century that I've lived here. When I arrived the sight of a kite was comparatively rare and certainly none bred in our valley. When Iolo first took me out to see the army surveillance operation in the Elan Valley there were just two pairs in West Radnorshire and the location of the nests was a closely-guarded secret for fear of egg thieves.

Things have been transformed since then. At first numbers built up slowly. It was a decade before they bred in my valley, although it is less than three miles from one of the two nests I visited with Iolo. His work was aided by a team of volunteers who would struggle to locate every Welsh nest. Everything was counted – even eggs – and nests deemed to be most at risk from egg collectors would be guarded. Just before fledging the young would be measured and weighed. Then much to the irritation of wildlife photographers, coloured tags would be clipped to their wings so future progress could be monitored from afar with binoculars.

Then their fortunes took off meteorically in the first decade of this century. This was partially natural because numbers reached a critical mass, but also thanks to feeding stations such as that at Gigrin on the other side of my mountain. This visitor attraction on the outskirts of Rhayader now attracts up to five hundred kites each afternoon and there are dozens of pairs in my valley, with two pairs nesting on my smallholding alone. Not surprisingly the conservationists have given up counting and are content to estimate the population at around one thousand pairs.

As numbers have increased so these icons of Mid-Wales have become more conspicuous and started to roost communally in winter. These would be in favourite trees - usually an oak or ash and for some reason they often appear to prefer a struggling tree with dead branches near the crown, no doubt because this makes for an ideal vantage point. One particular favourite is a half-dead oak on the main road at the bottom of the hill, but there is another in a huge ash near the top of the back lane into Rhayader. At first these roosts would be limited to four or five birds and they were clearly jumpy about the presence of humans for they would all leave their perches as the car approached, even when it was almost completely dark, flying off to circle in the night sky.

Slowly these roosts have built up to forty or fifty strong and they are markedly more comfortable with the presence of humans, often not bothering to take off as the car drives past and they will happily fly relatively close when I am walking on the hill, particularly if the hawk is on my fist.

Over the last couple of decades local wildlife seems to have become far more comfortable living alongside man. As far as I know there were no resident barn owls at Tan y Cefn when I moved here, now we have a breeding pair with one sufficiently at ease with my presence that she will take food from my palm. Most of the bird boxes I have put up around the house are occupied each spring and even the weasel seems comfortable with my presence – two nights ago she virtually ran over my foot when I opened the back door.

Living in Mid-Wales for a quarter of a century will never make me local, but I qualify as an incomer rather than outsider. As I type I am watching the male barn owl flying purposefully through the gloom towards the hay meadow while his mate incubates a clutch of seven eggs. I am hefted to my corner of West Radnorshire hillside. I also know the genuine meaning of the word cynefin.

ACKNOWLEDGEMENTS

This book could not have been written without help. Iolo Williams and Tony Cross opened doors to Welsh birdlife and conservation politics. Vic Pardoe and David James provided historical insight. Helen Nakielny has been a constant source of eclectic snippets of natural history and her sons, William and Arthur, provided inspirational enthusiasm. Finally, thanks to Mick Felton for the original commission and Lucy Johnson for constructive friendly criticism.